This Book Belongs To :

....

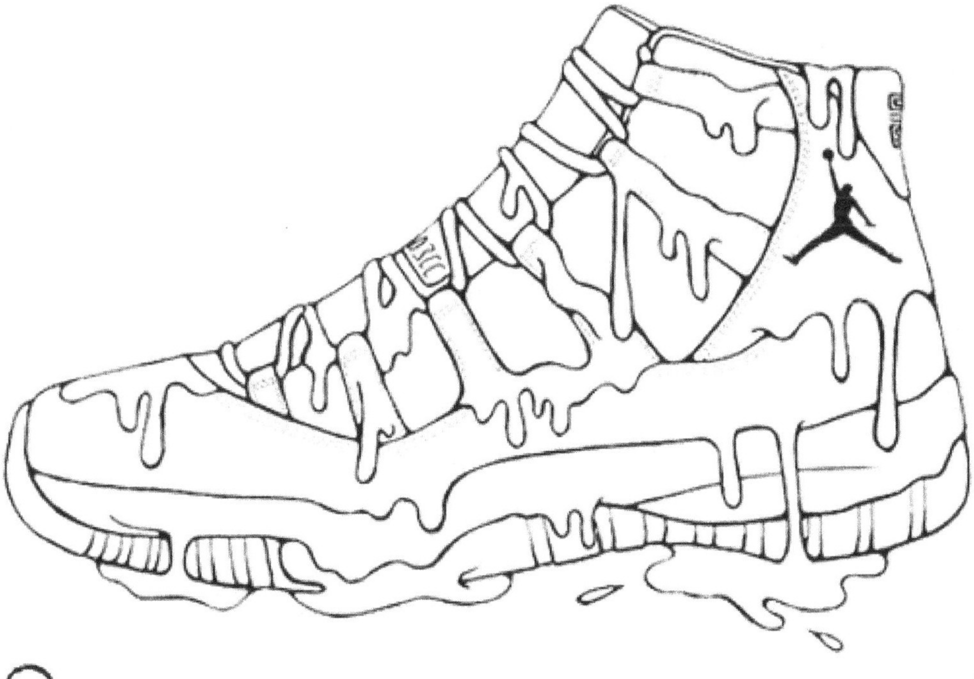

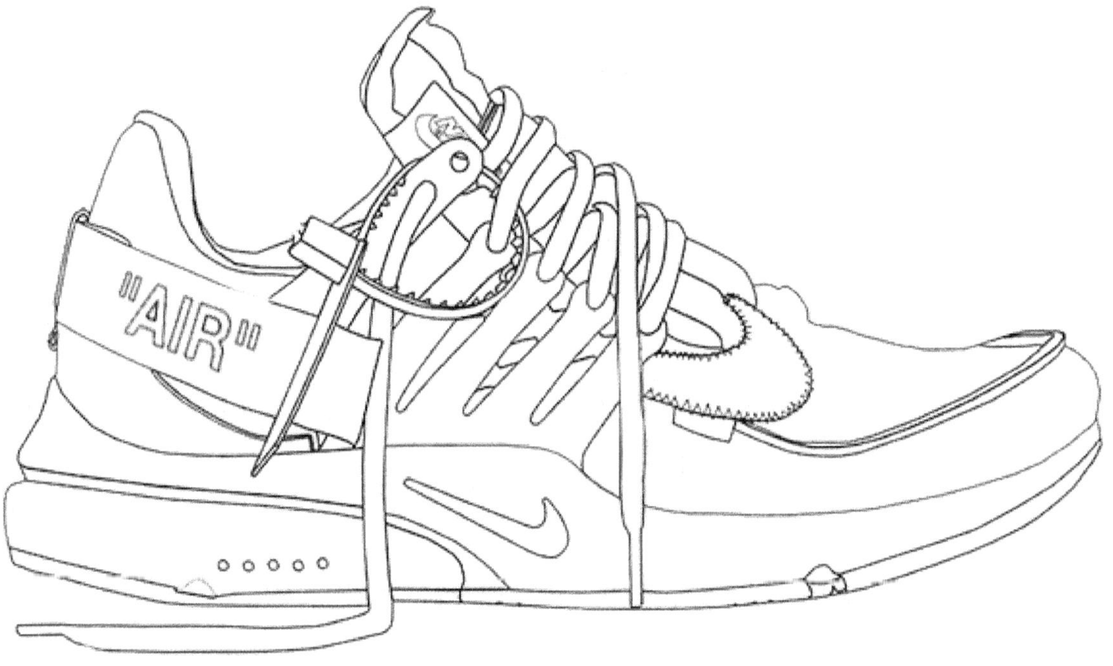
"AIR"

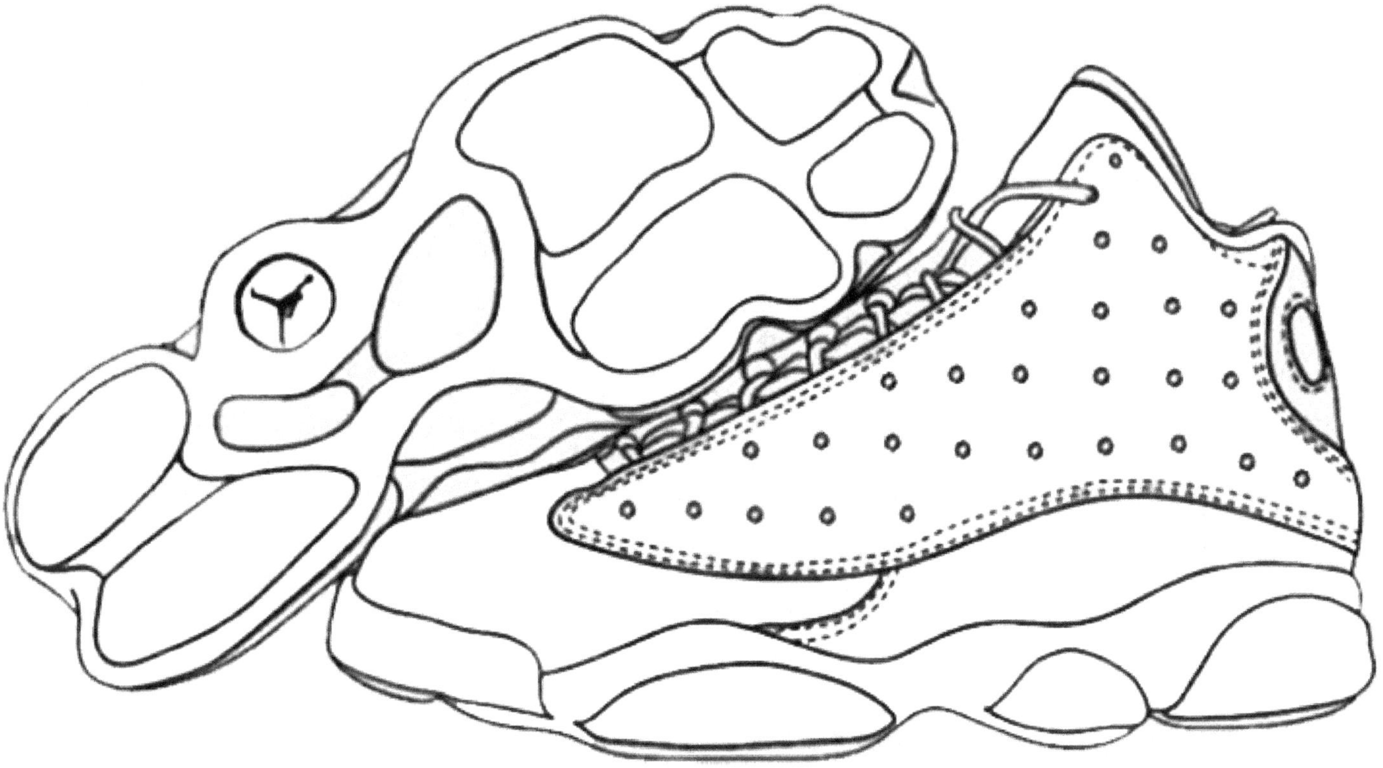

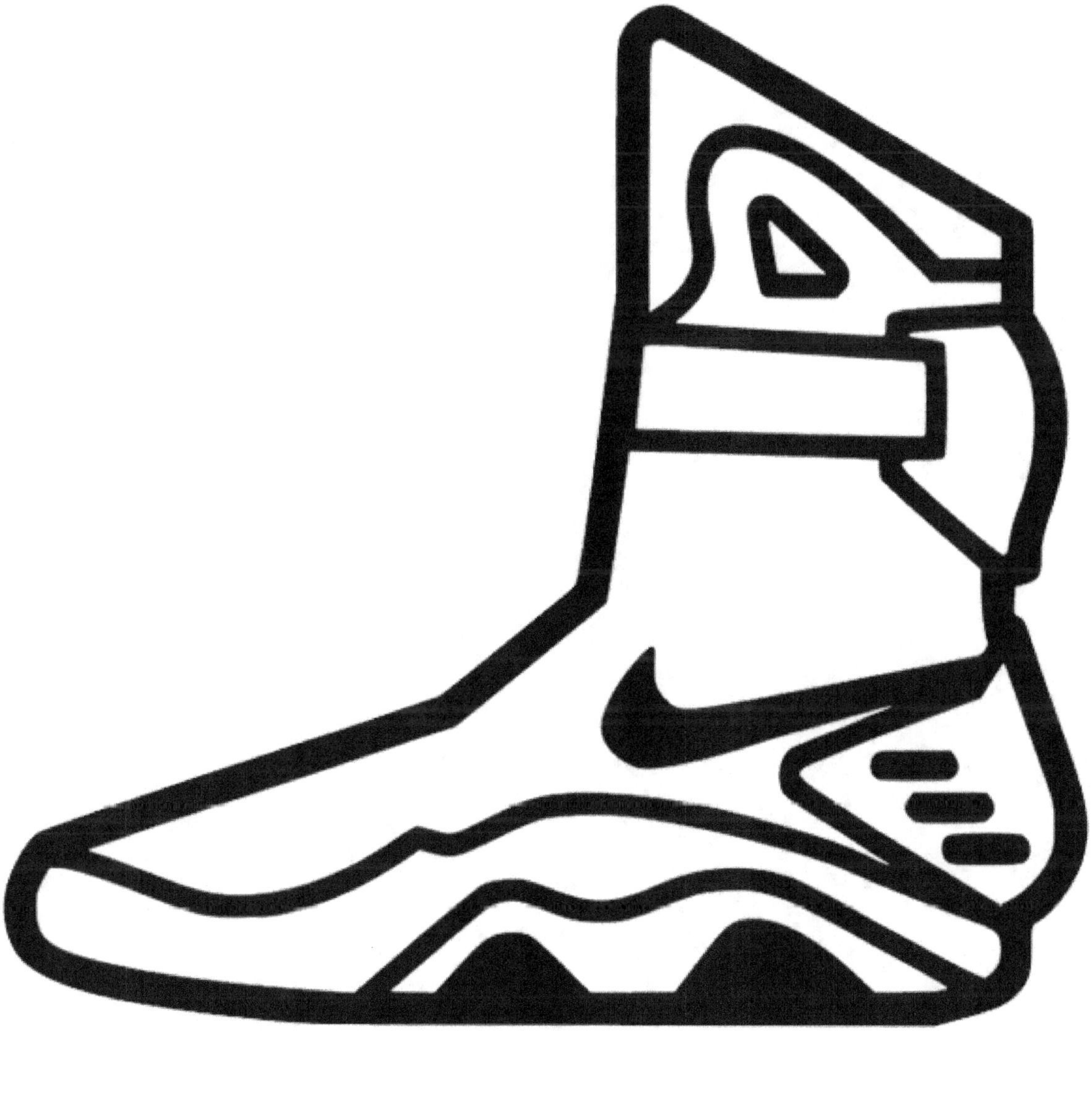

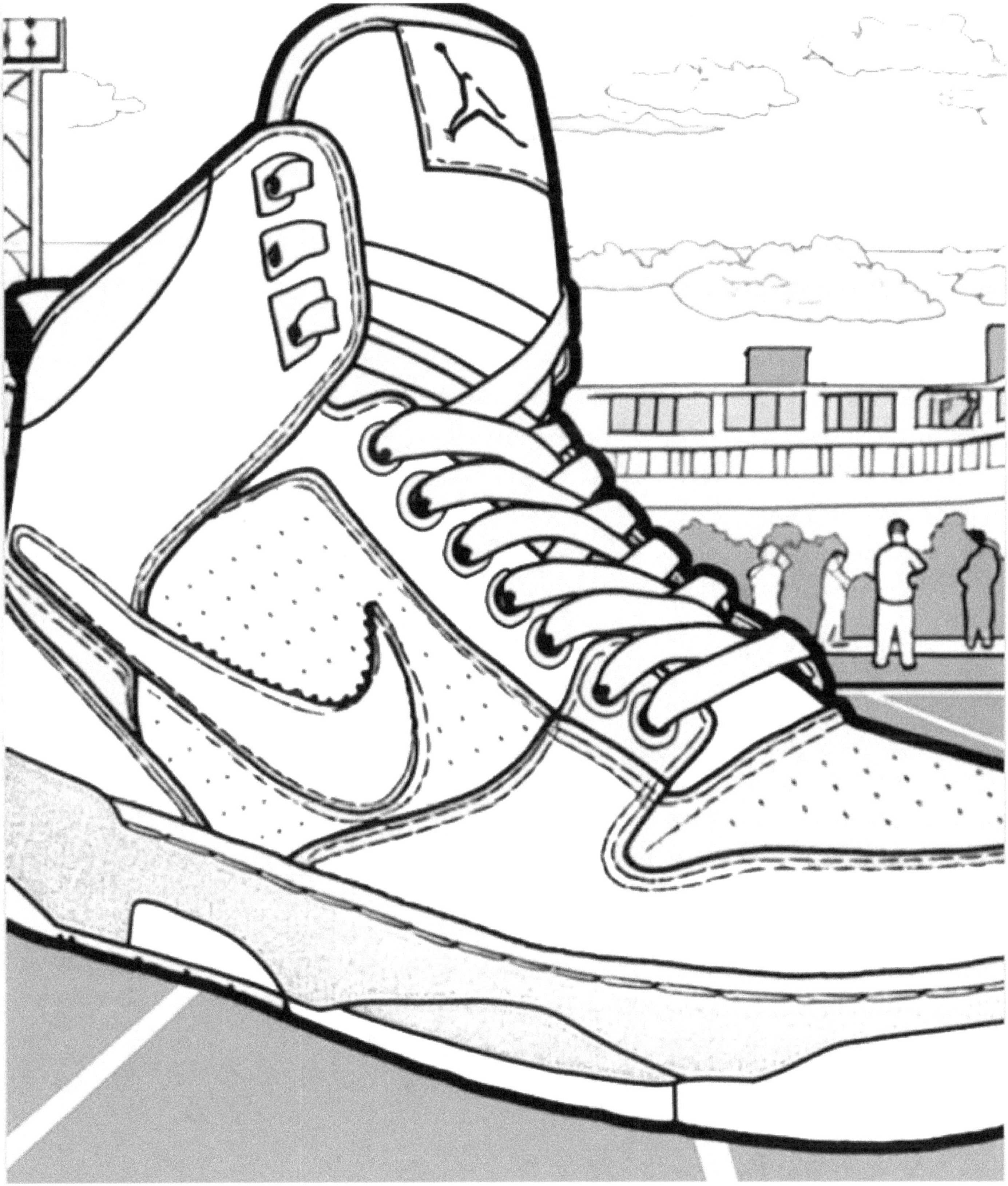

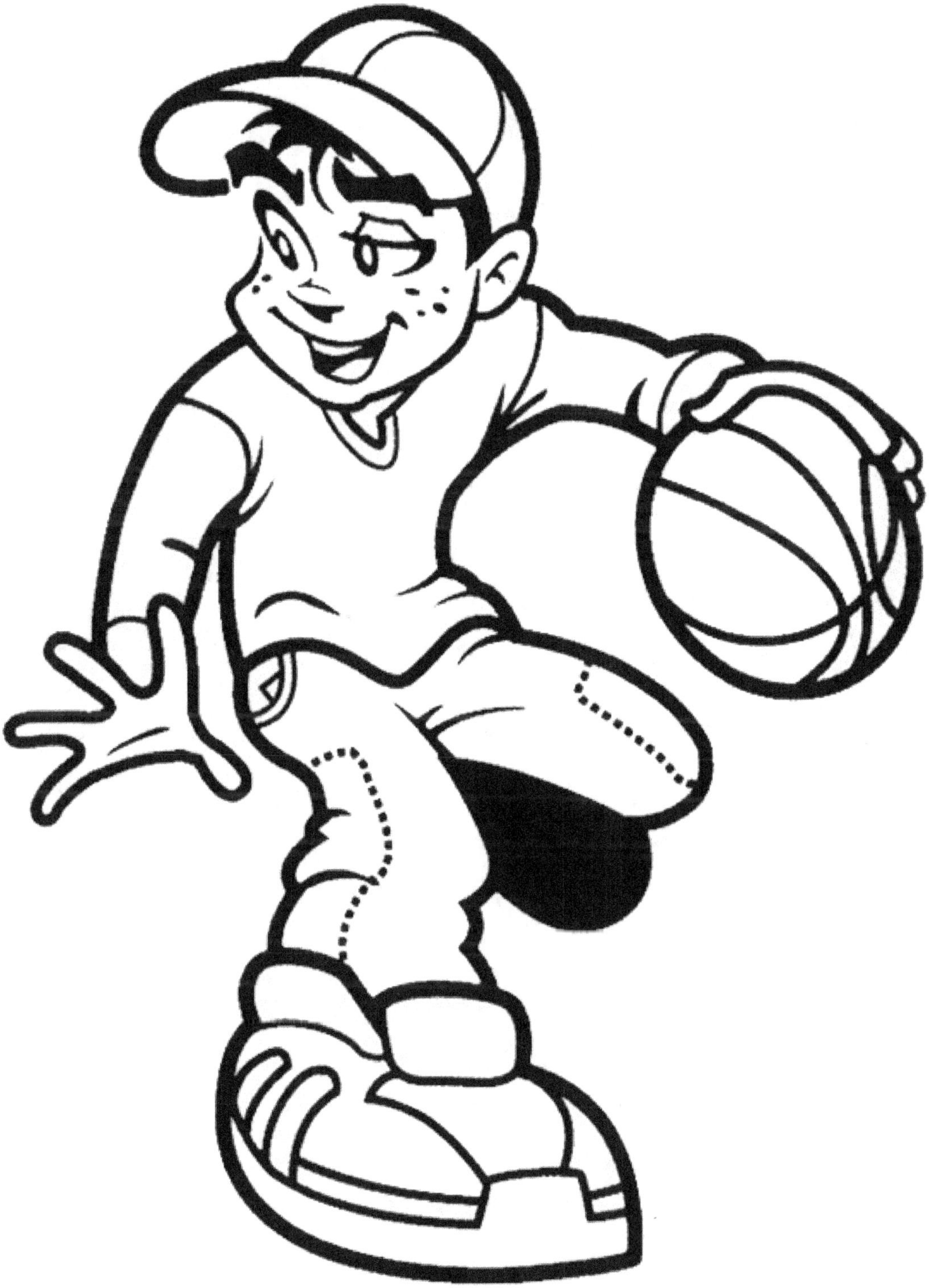

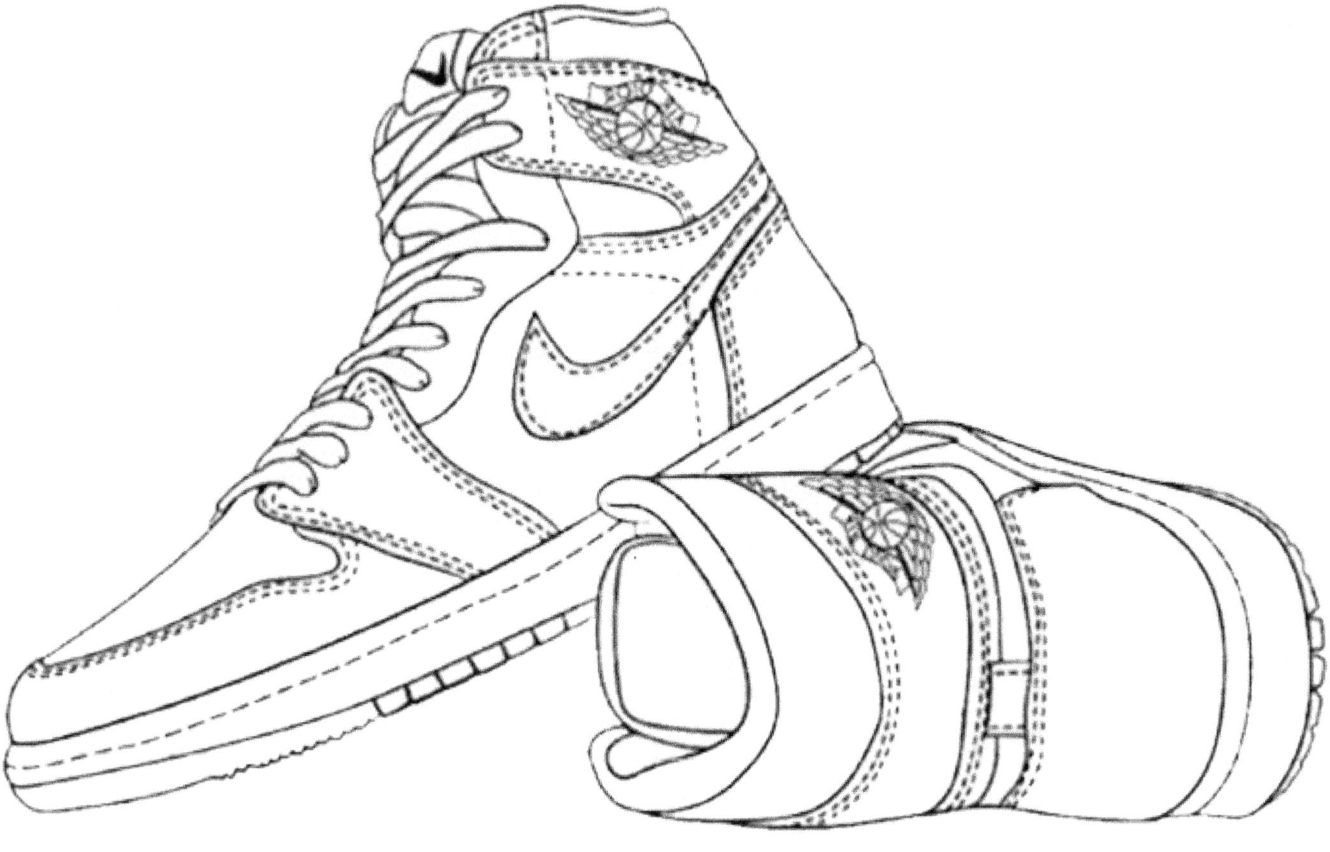

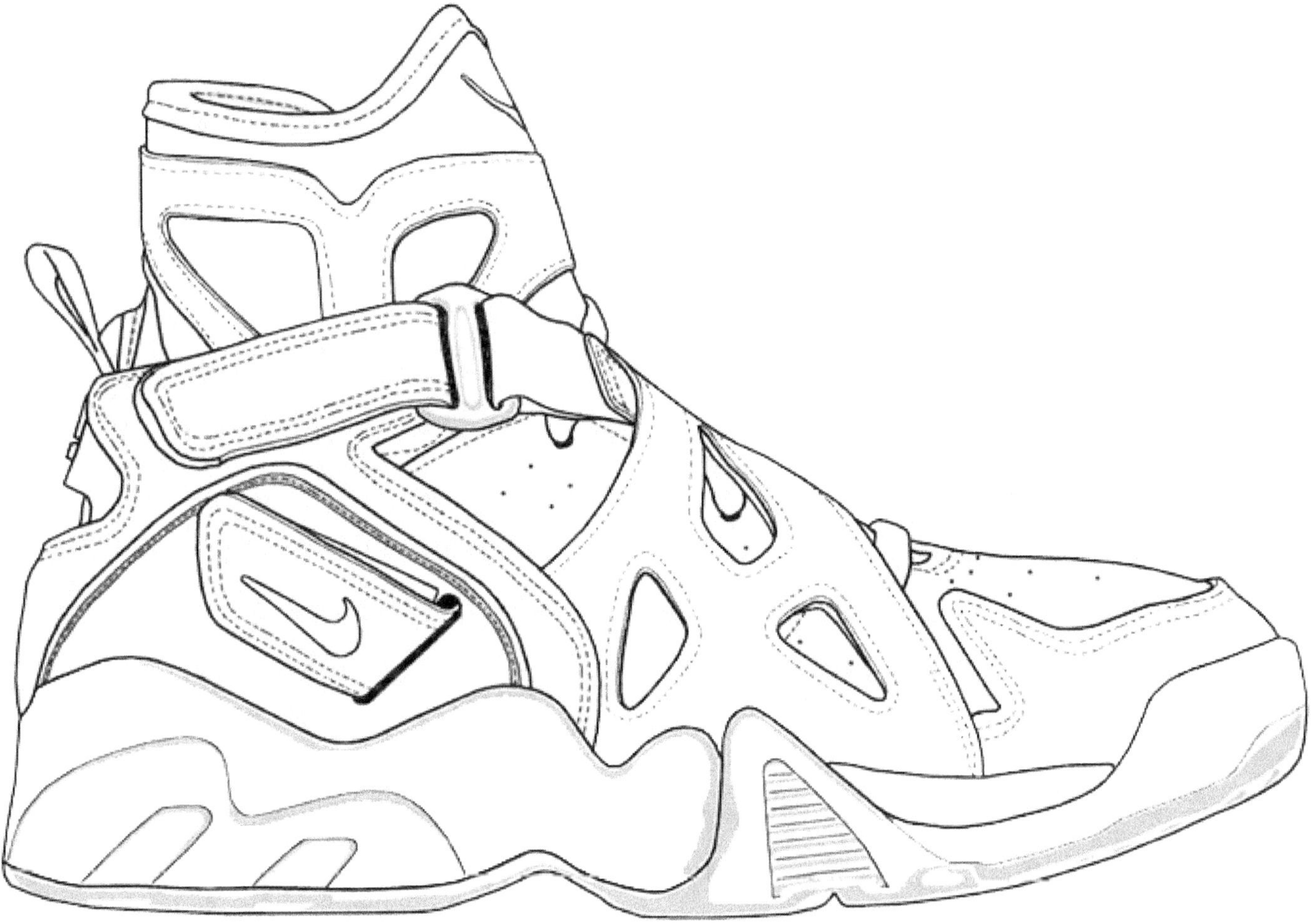

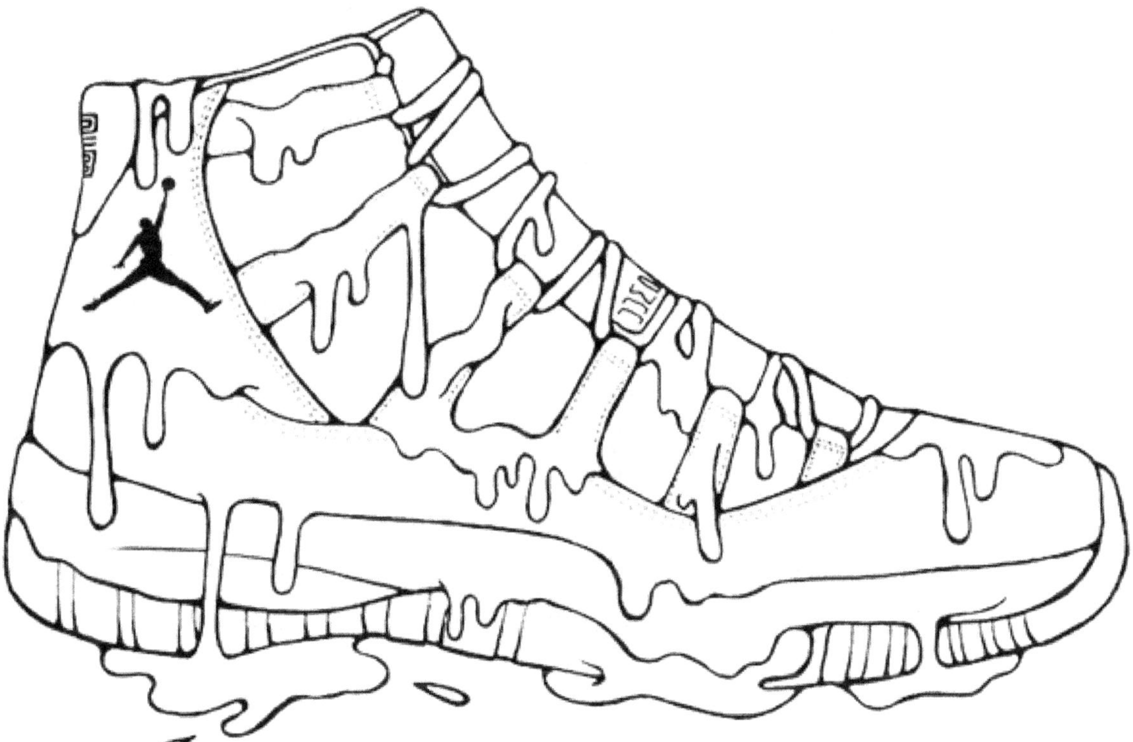

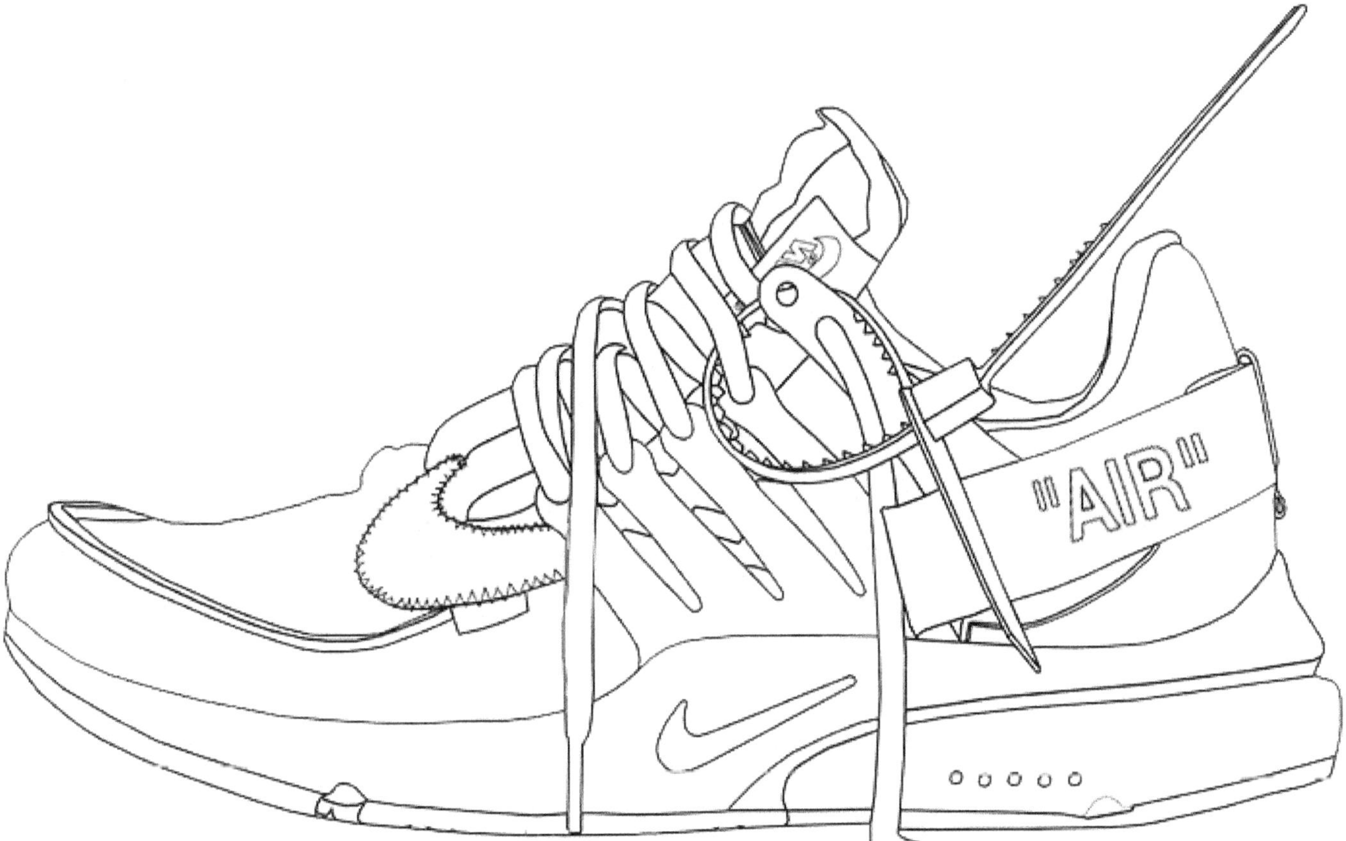
"AIR"

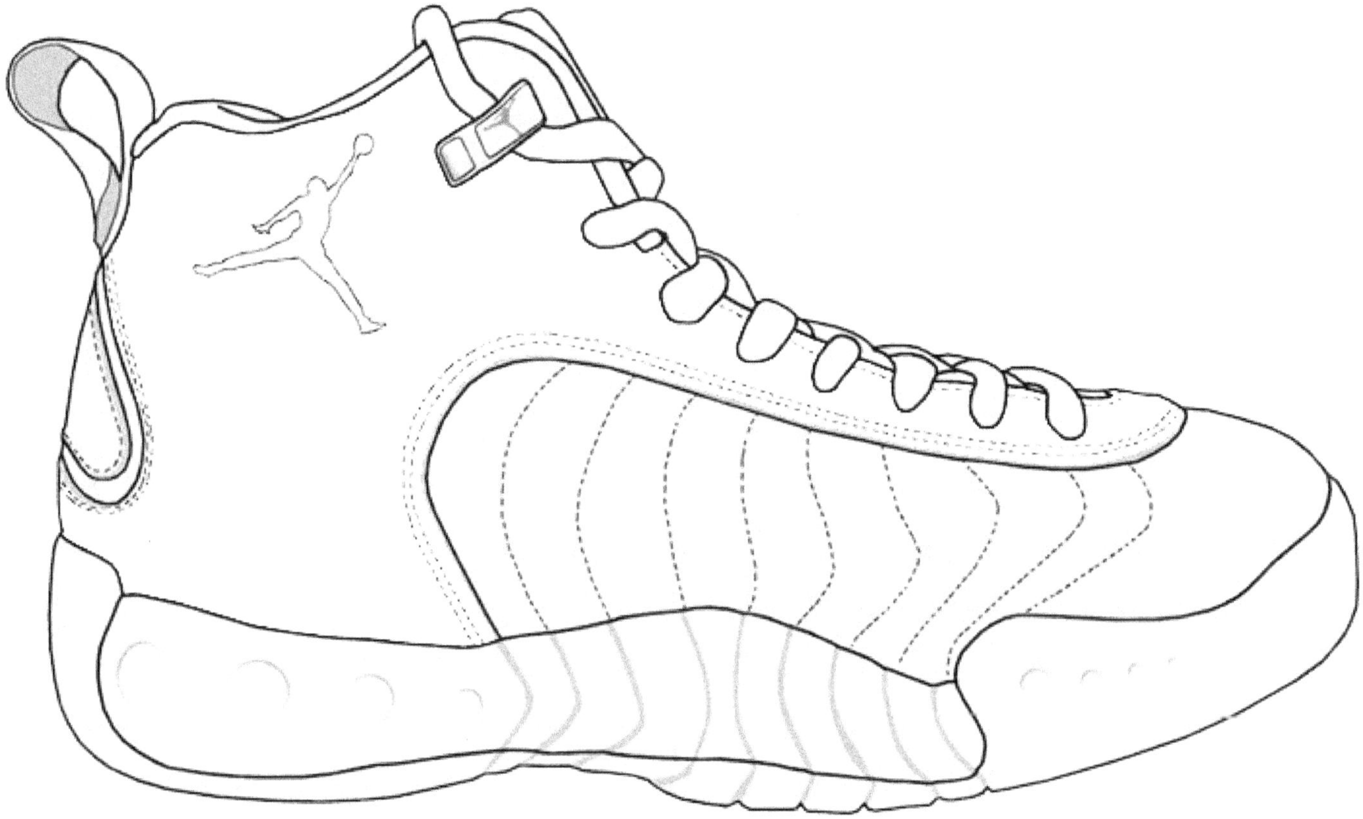

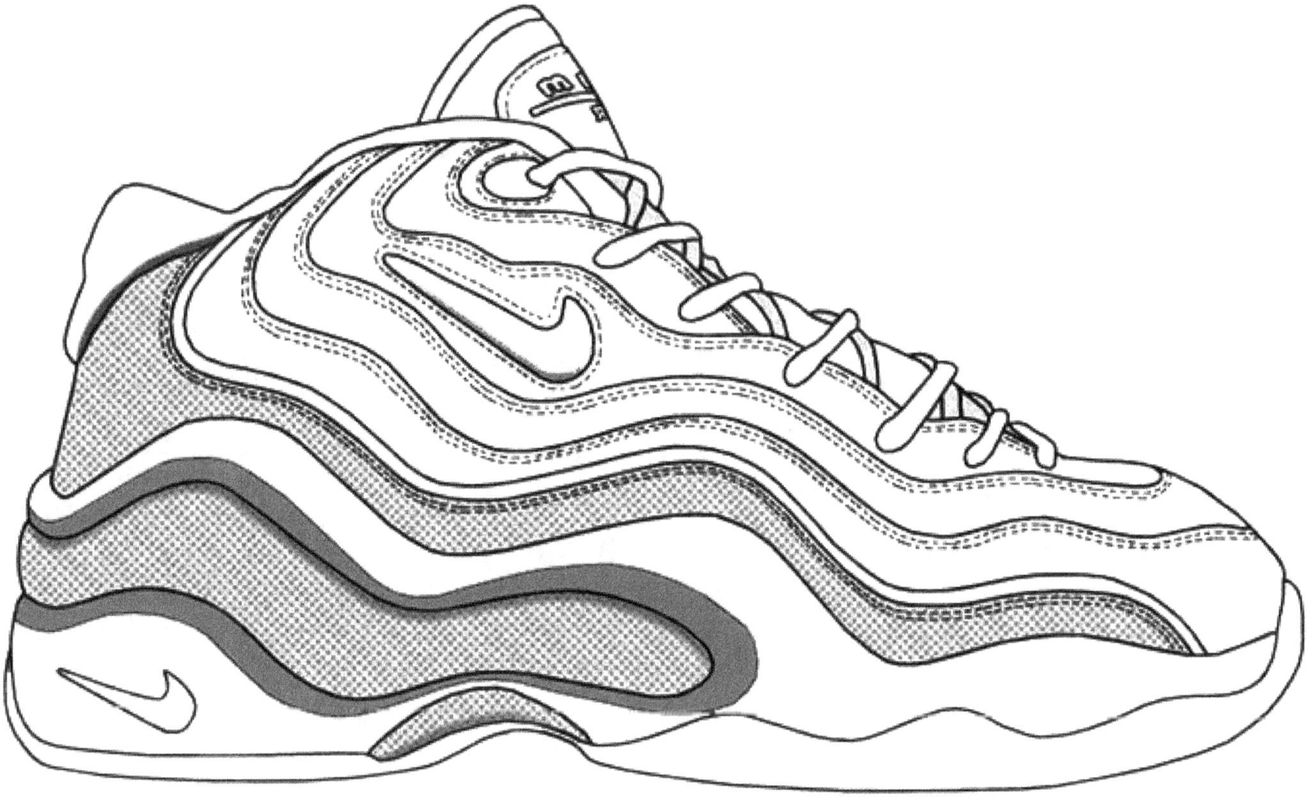

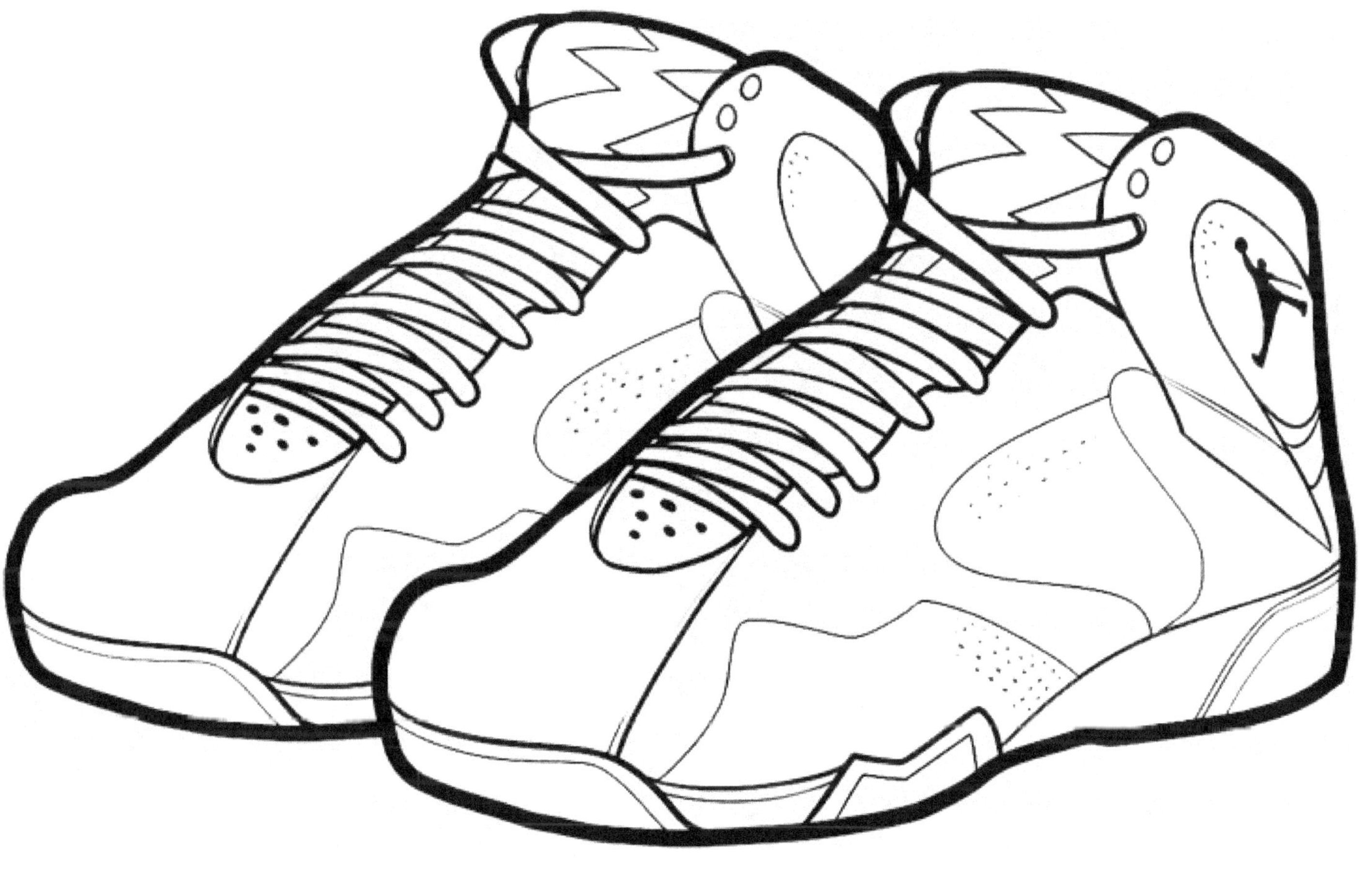

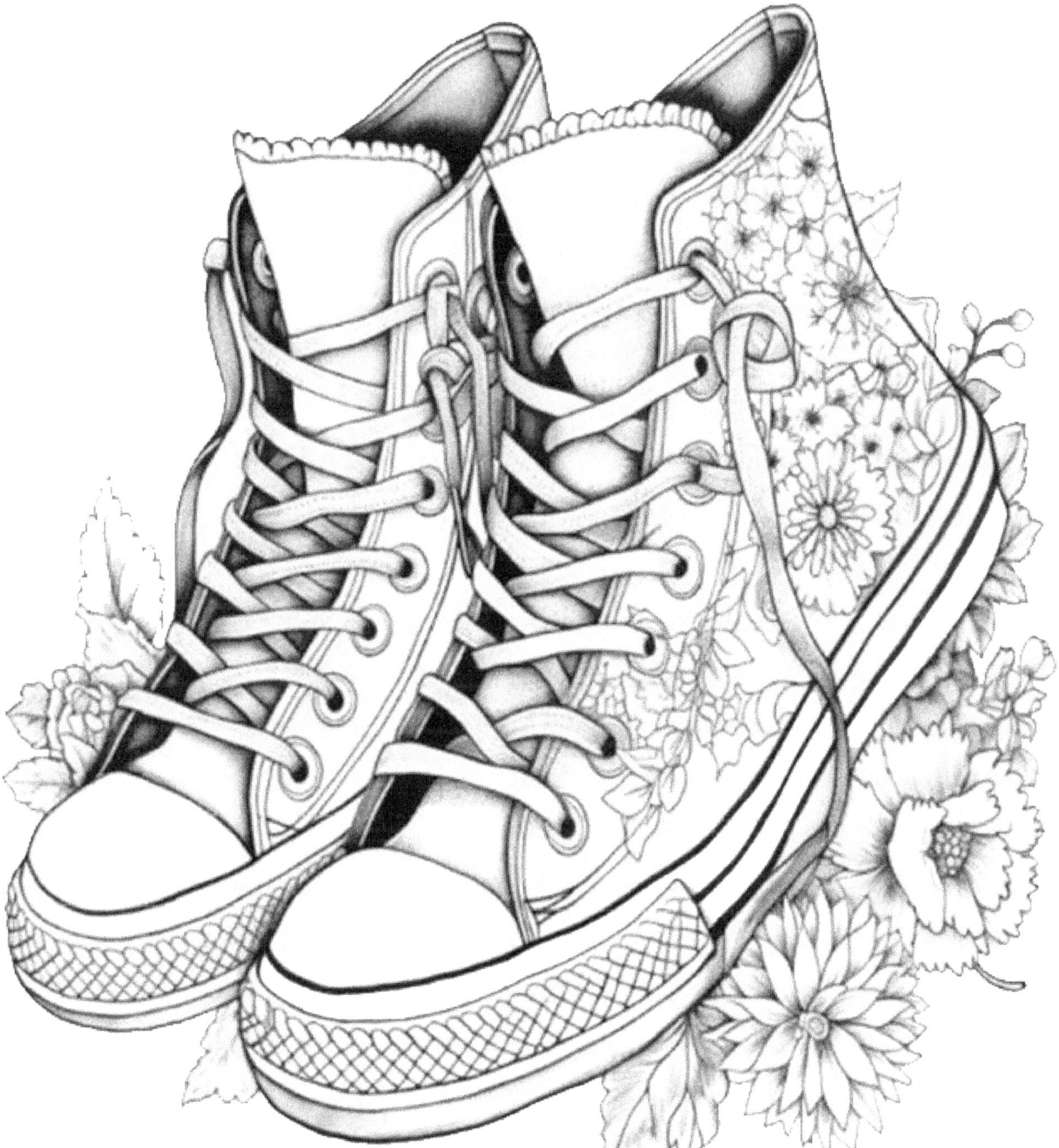

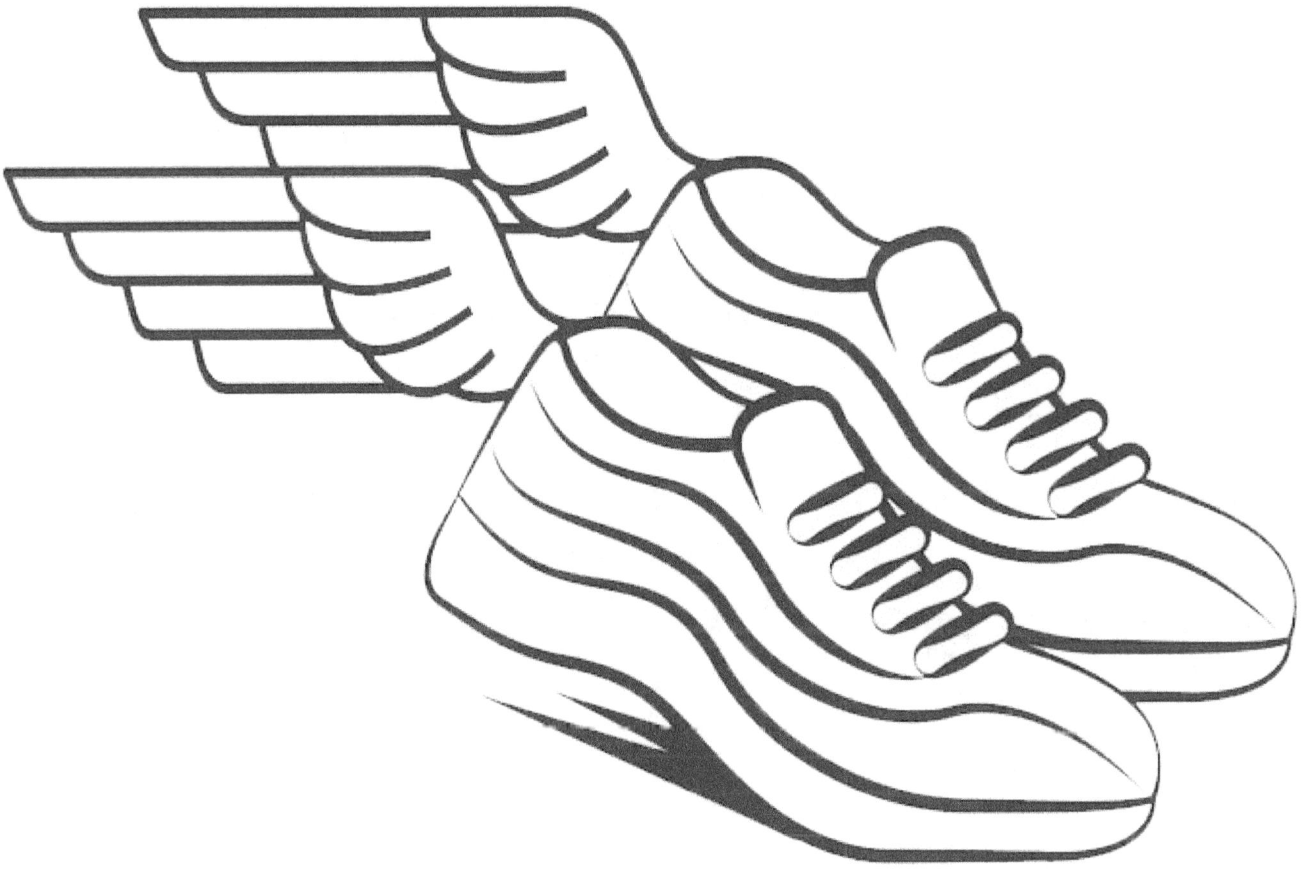

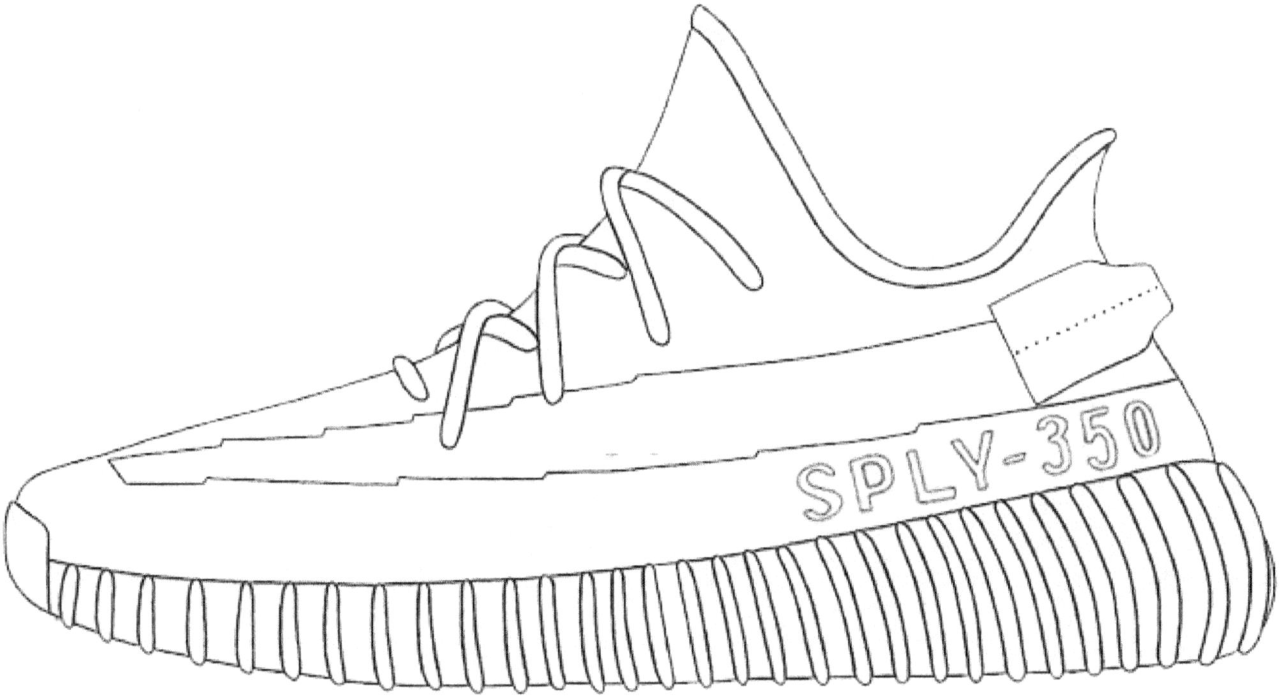
SPLY-350

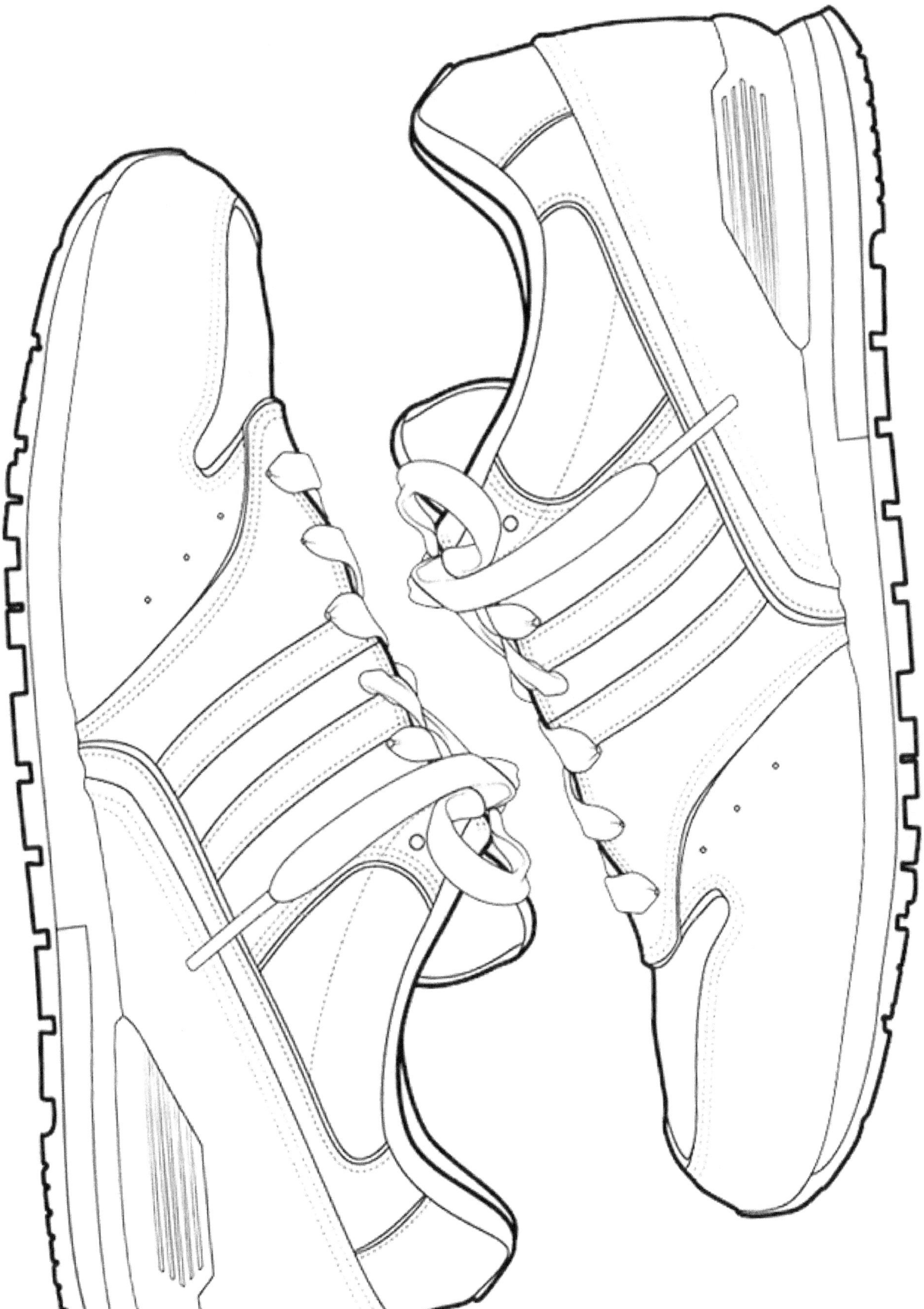

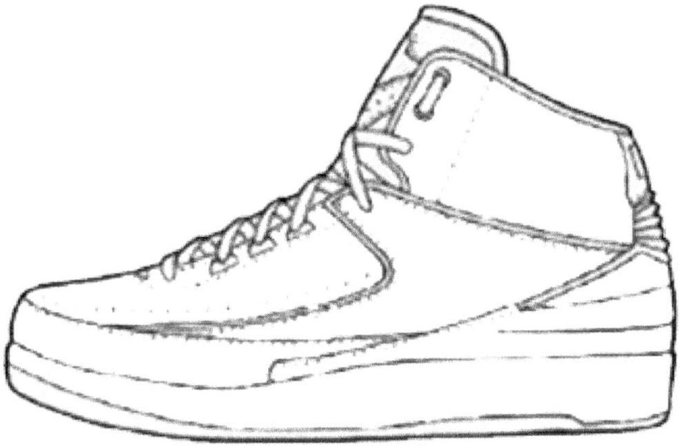
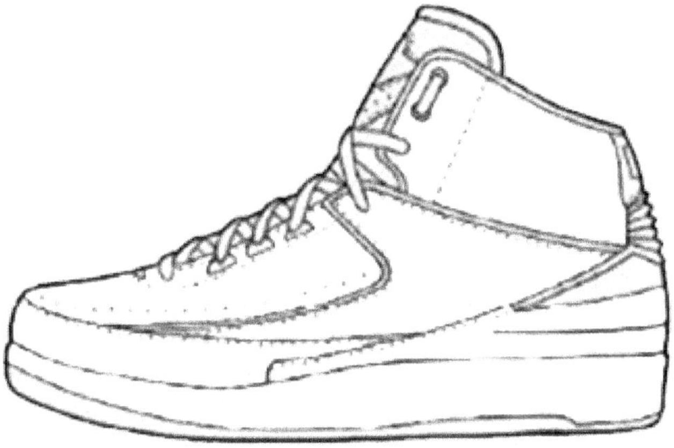
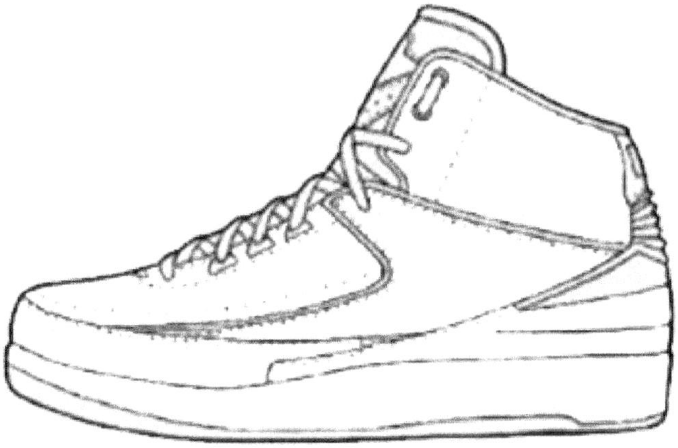
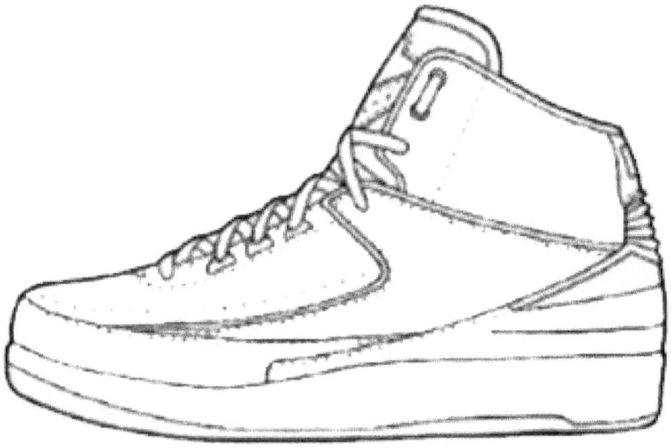
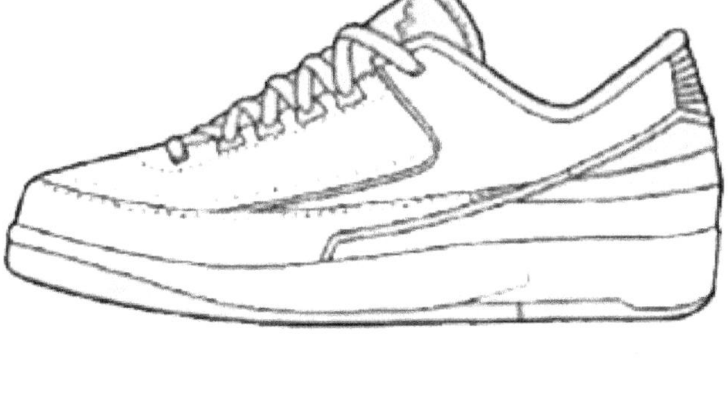
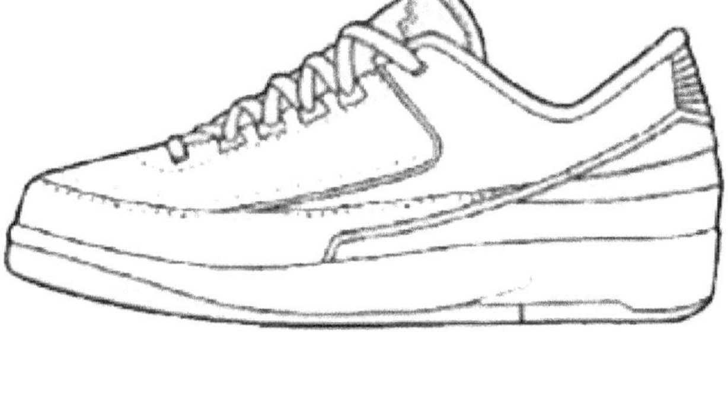

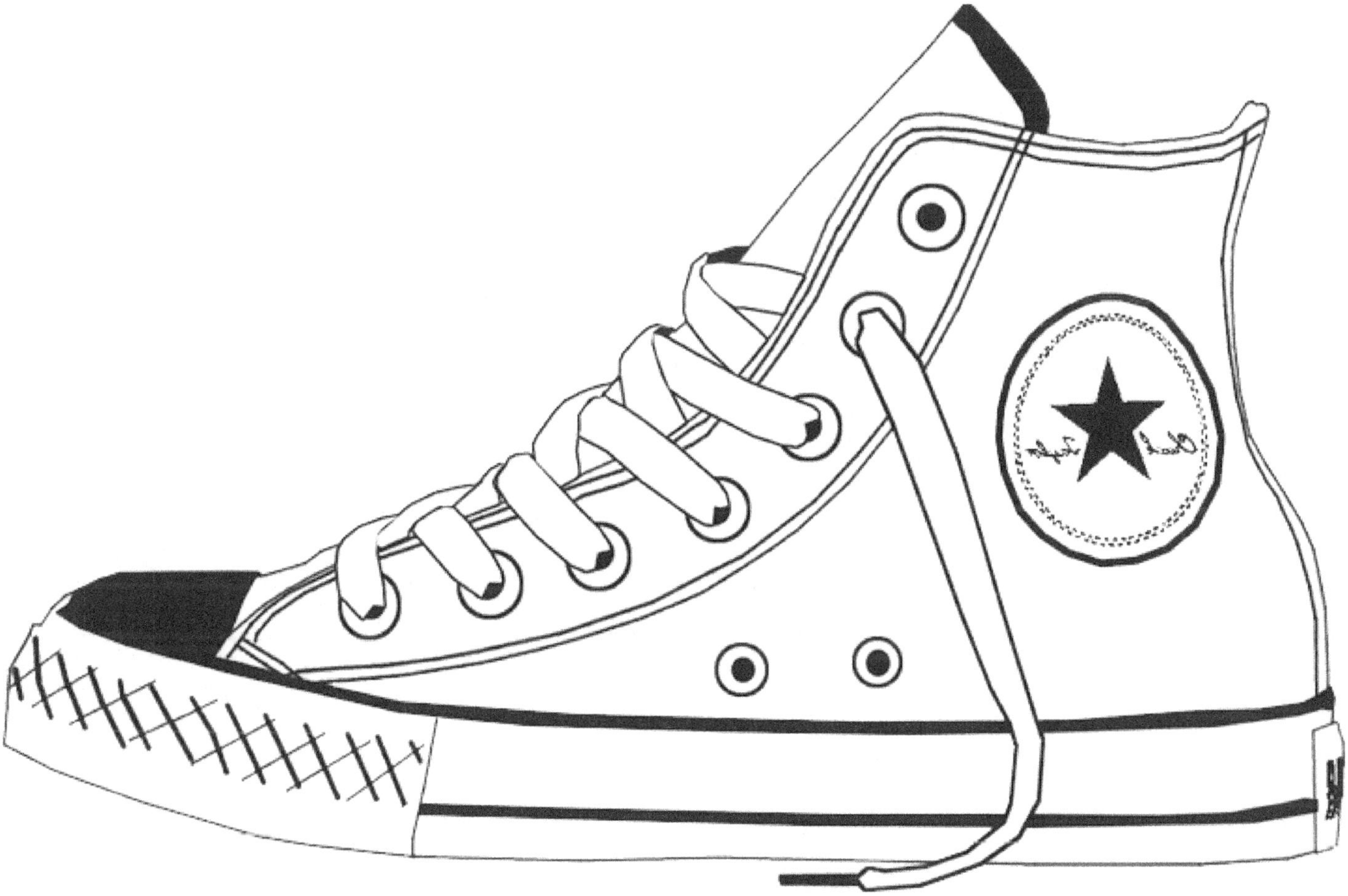

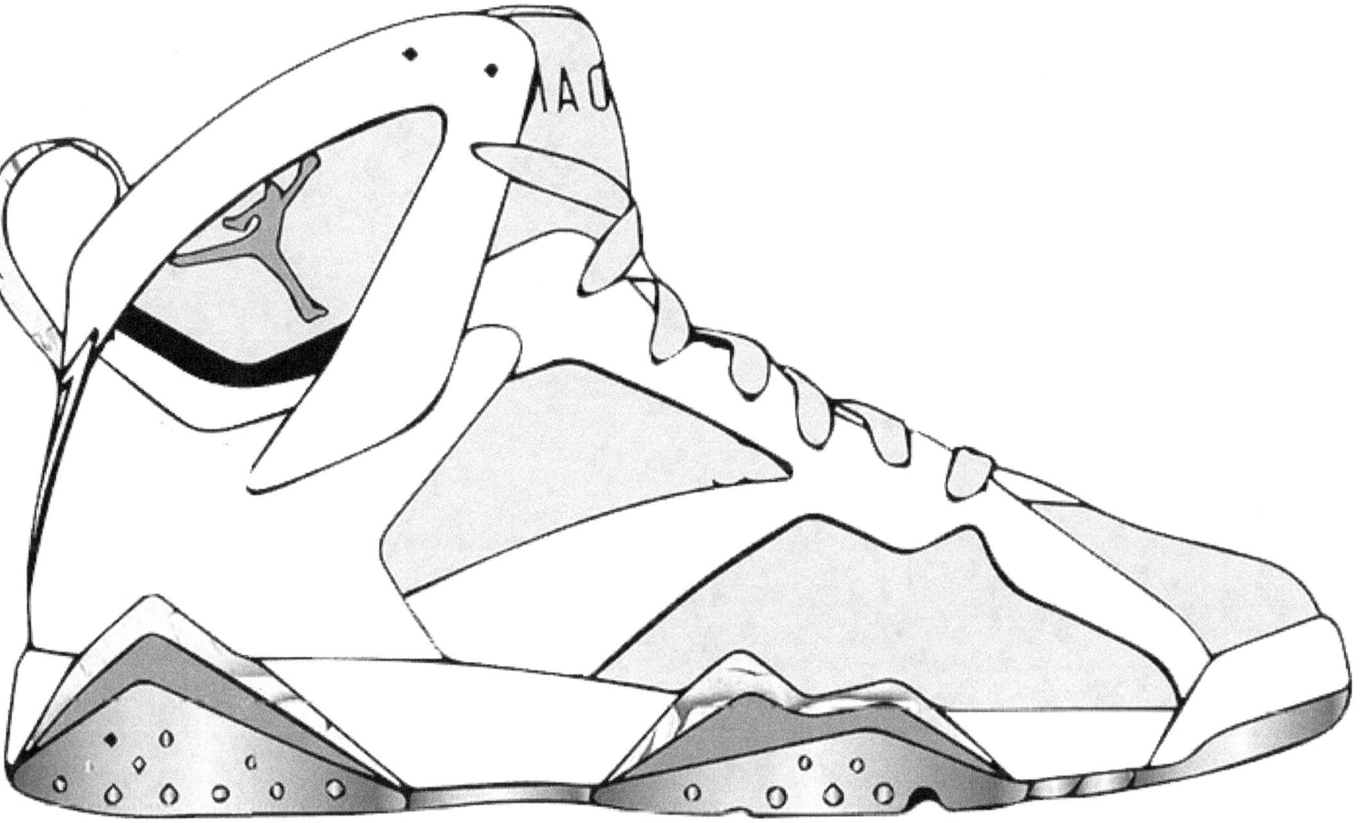

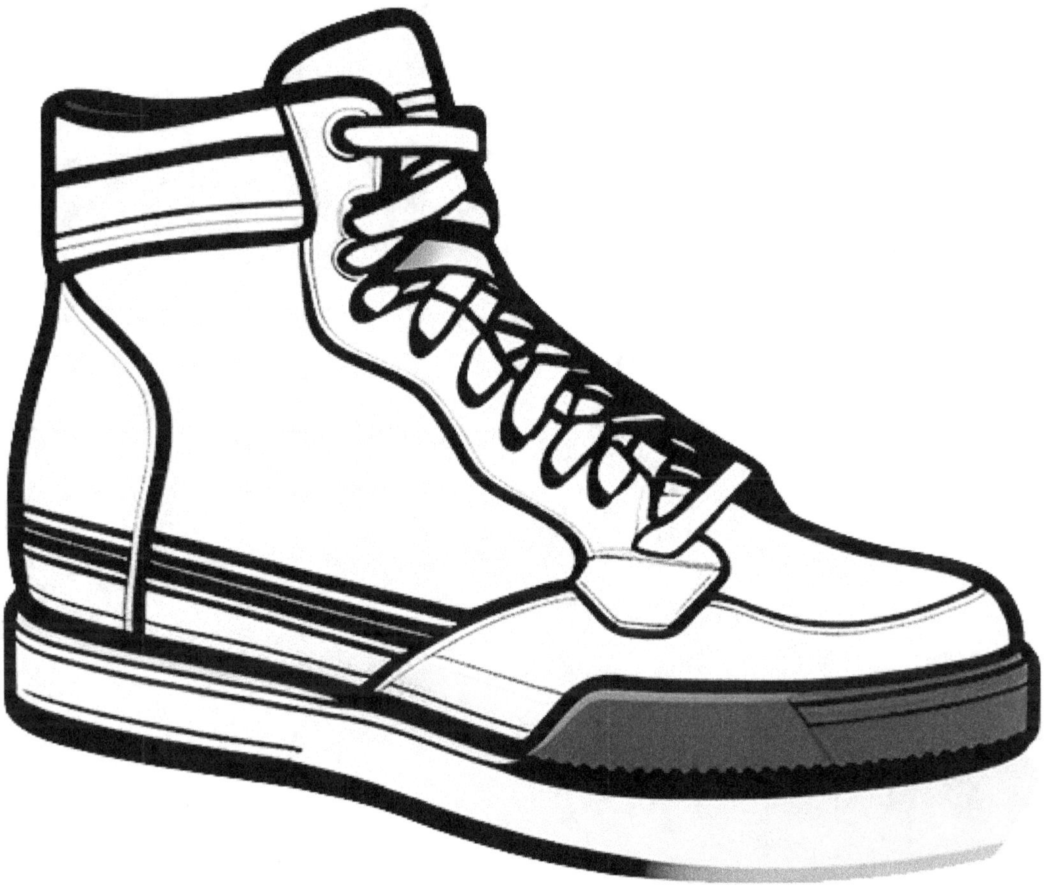
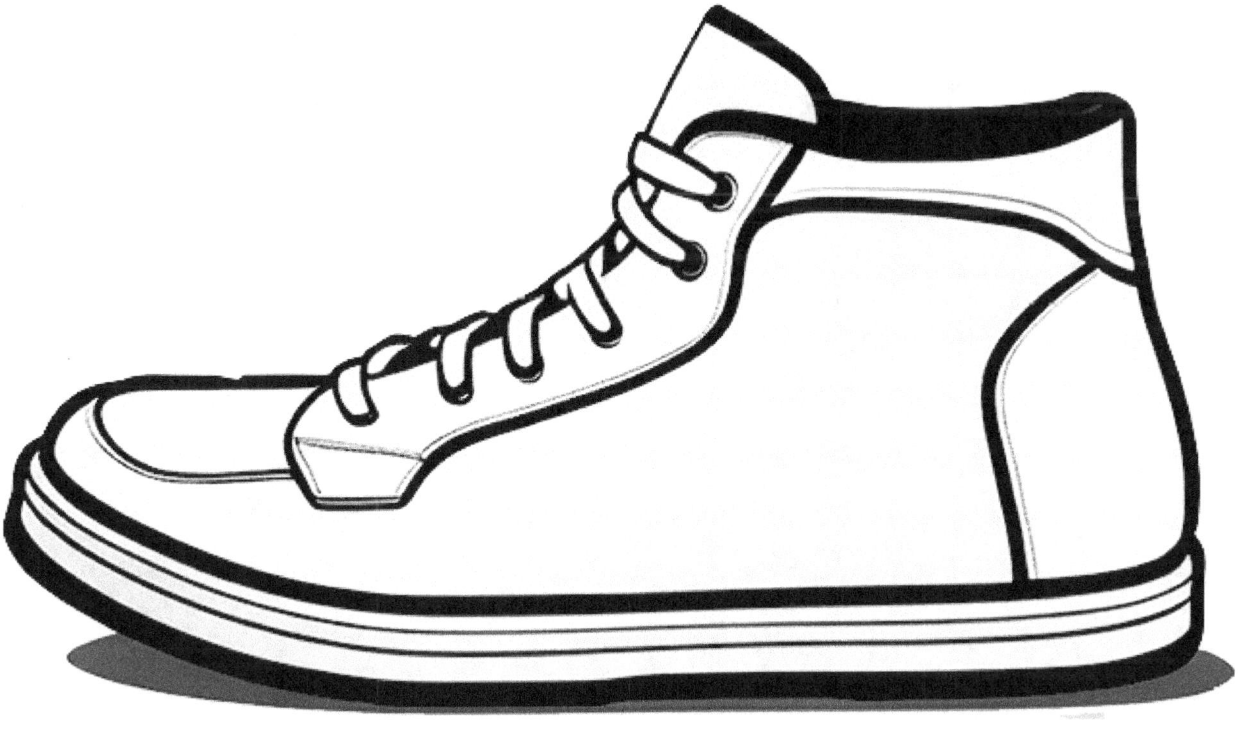

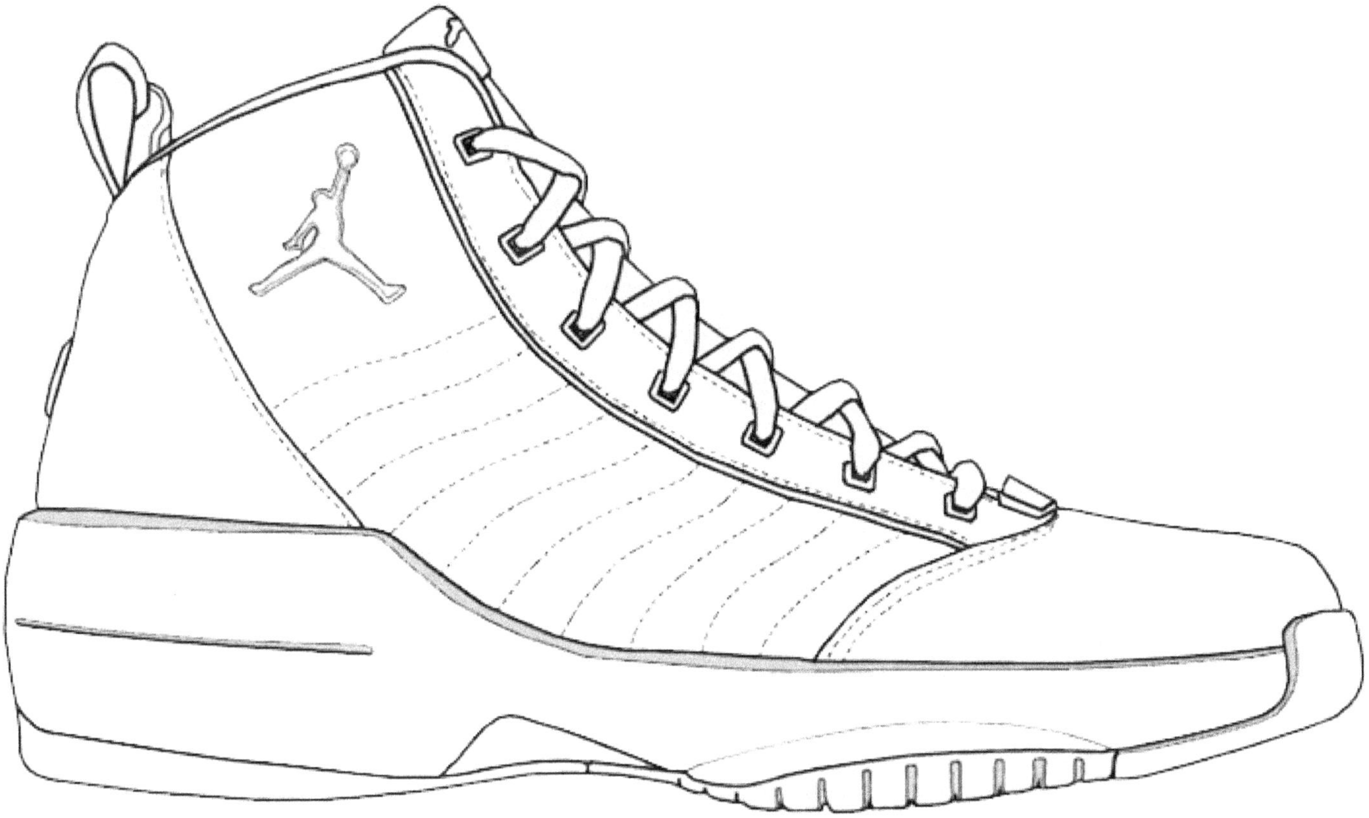

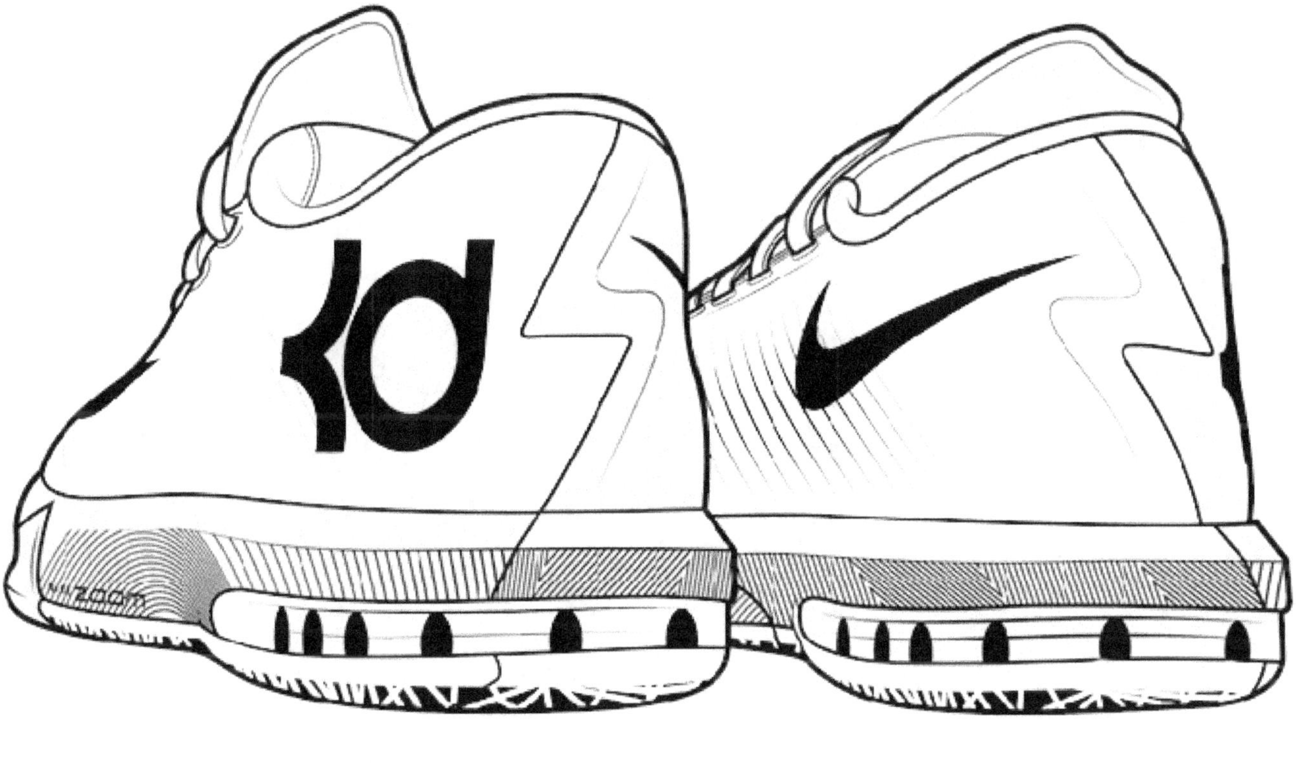
zoom

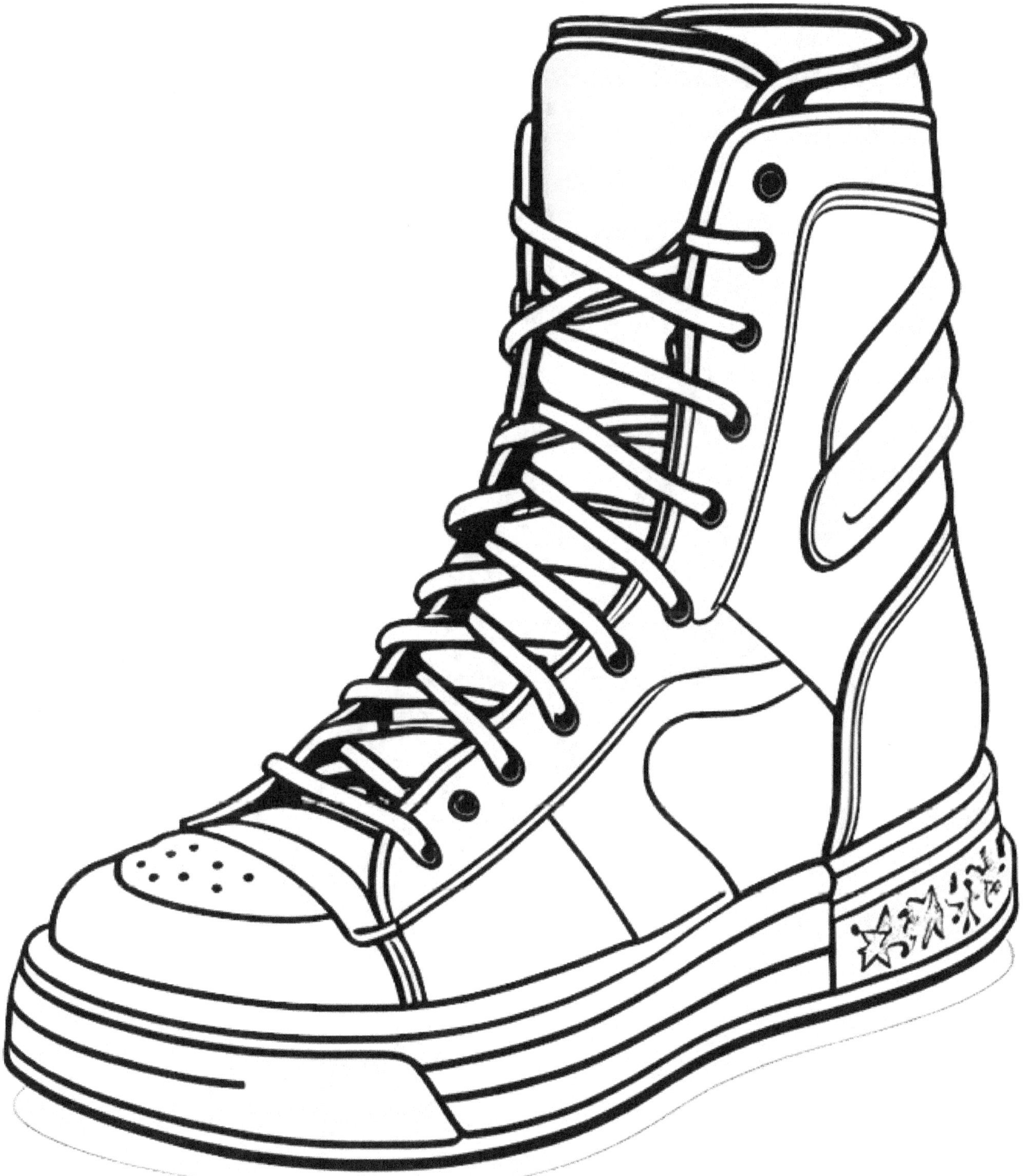

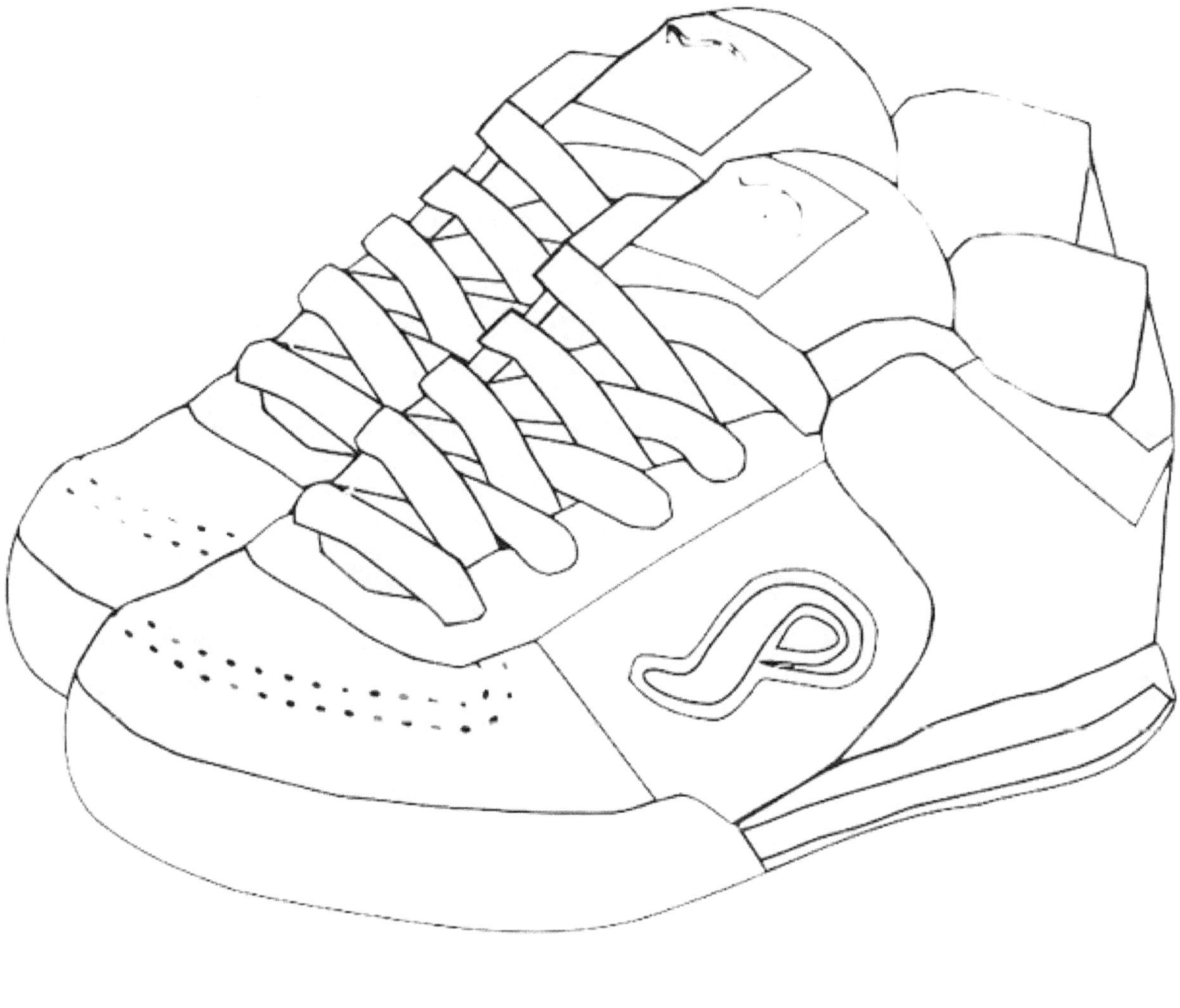

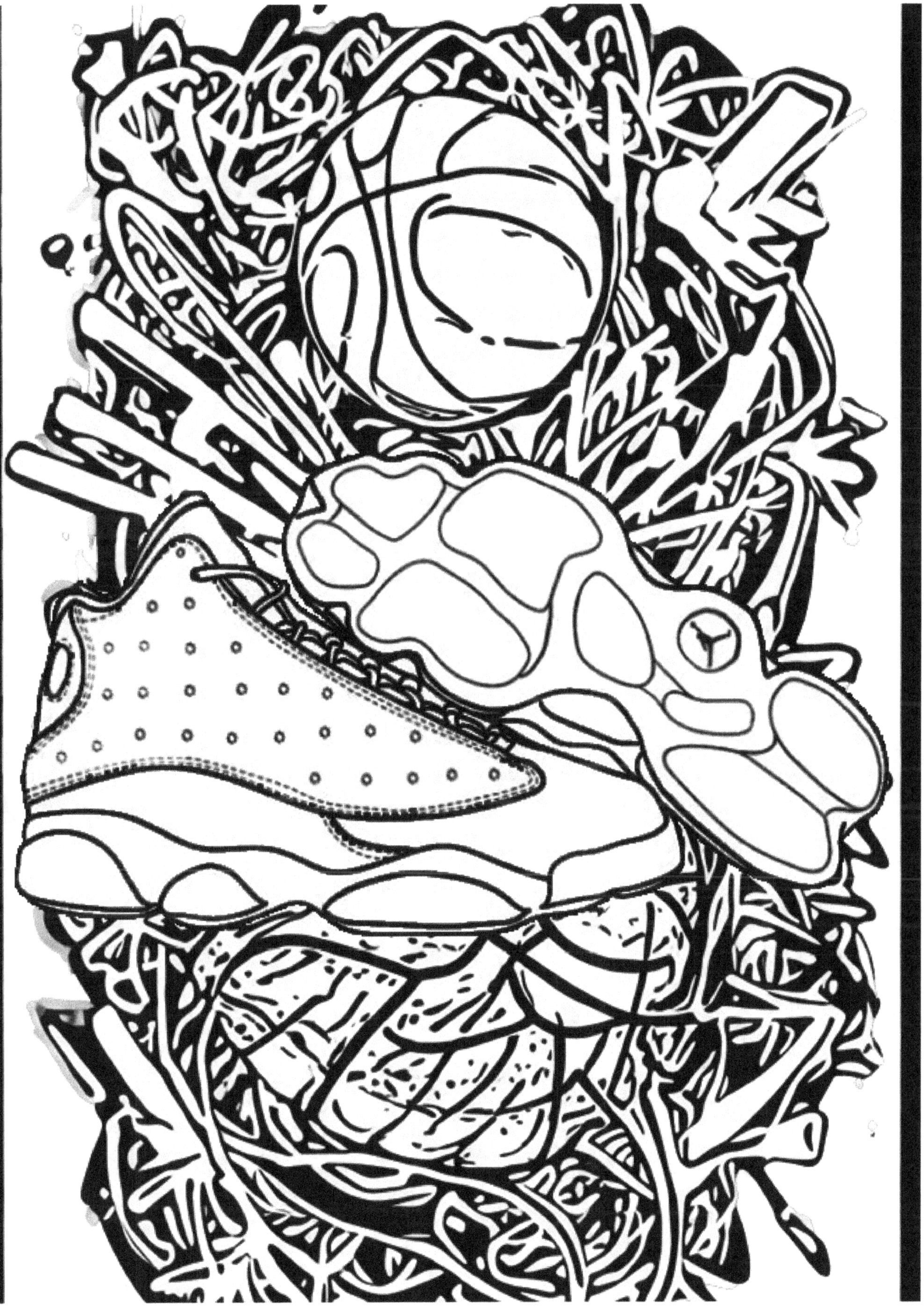

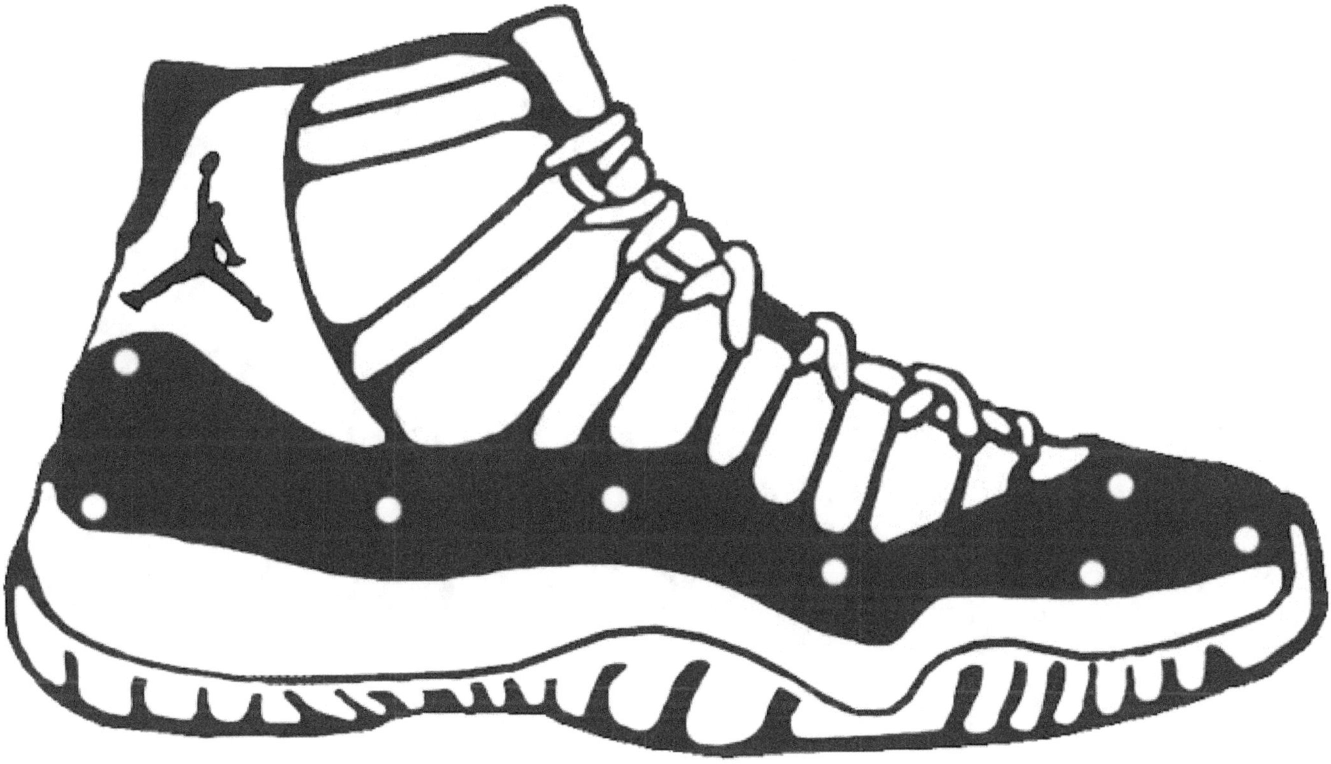

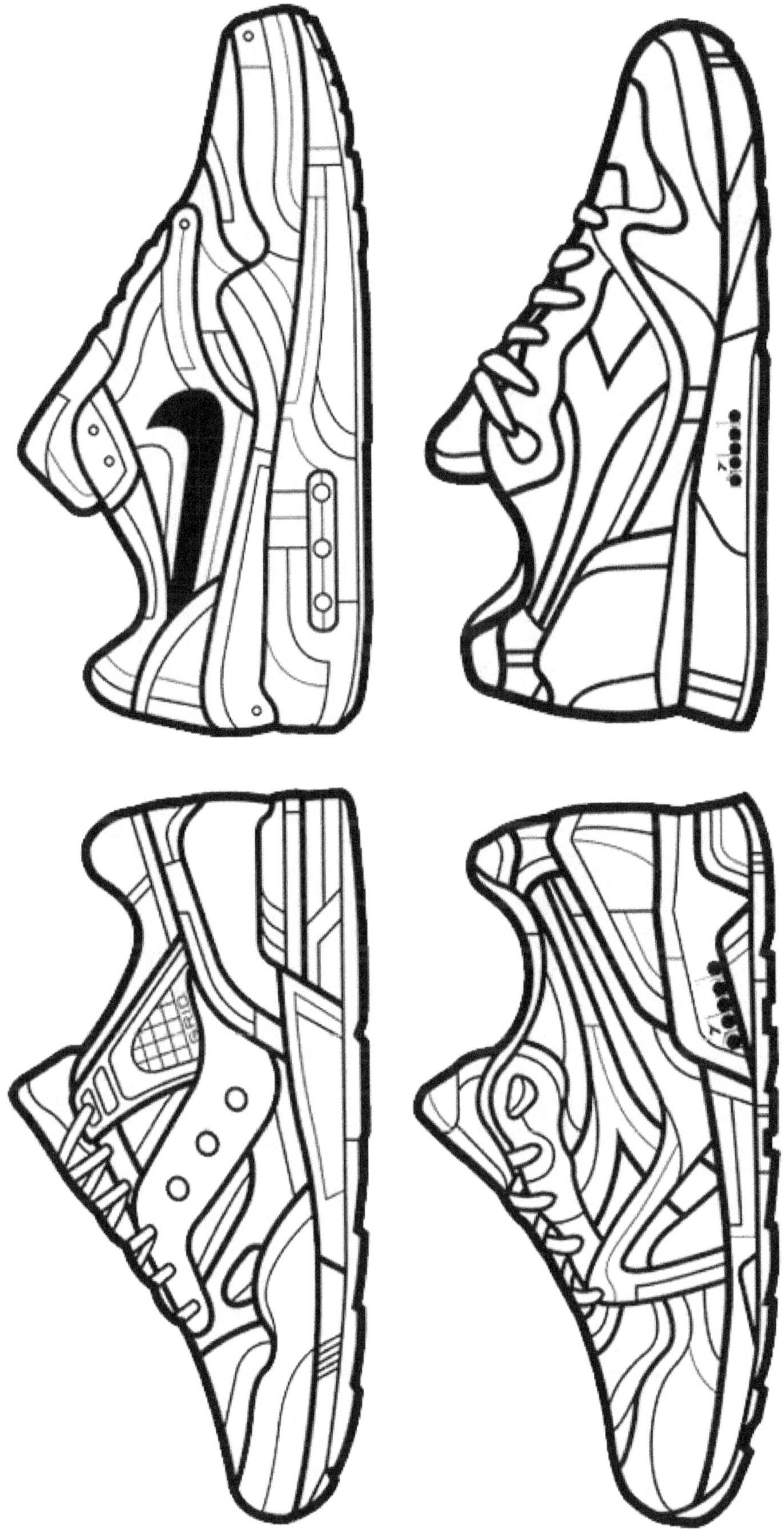

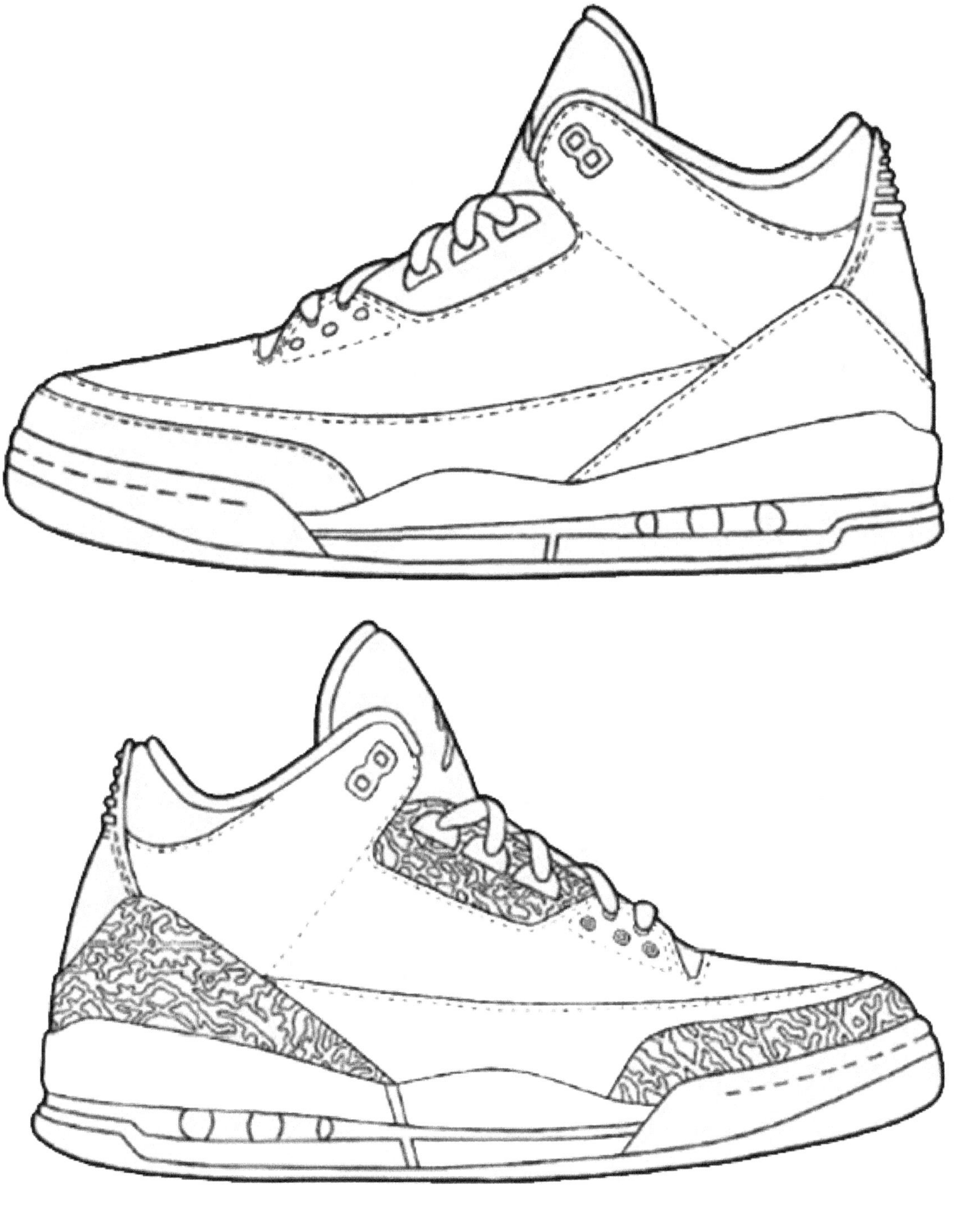

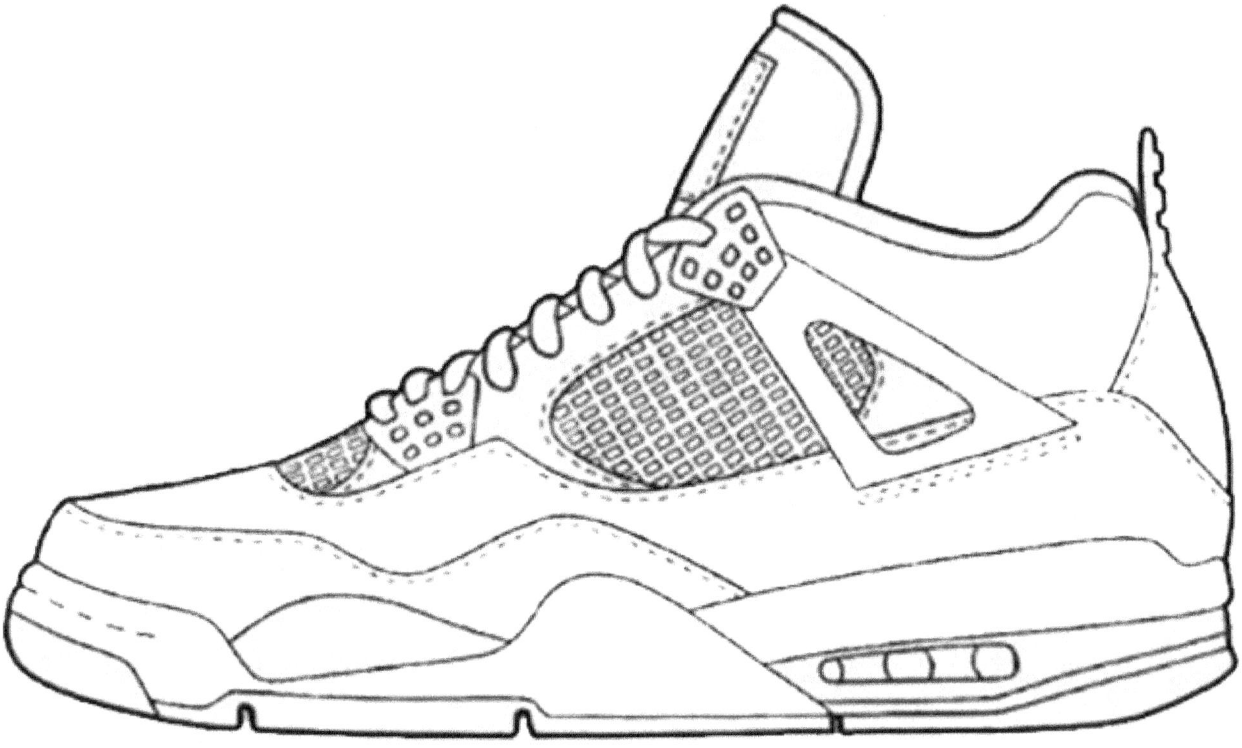

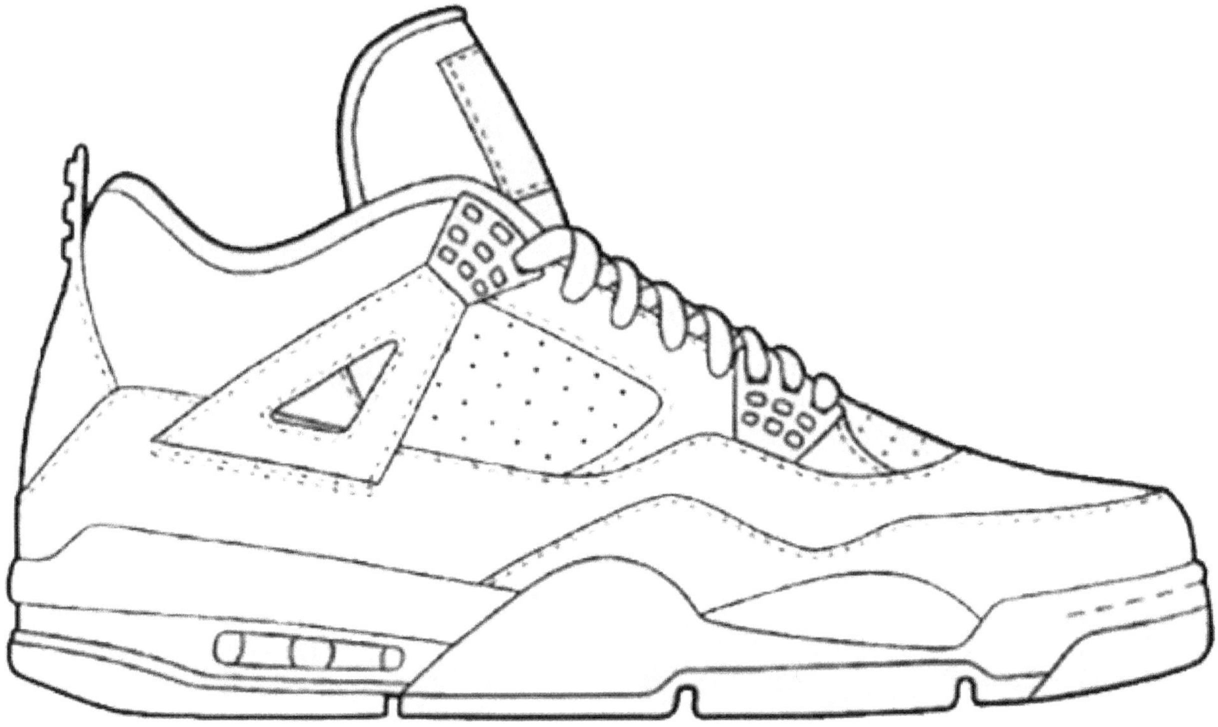

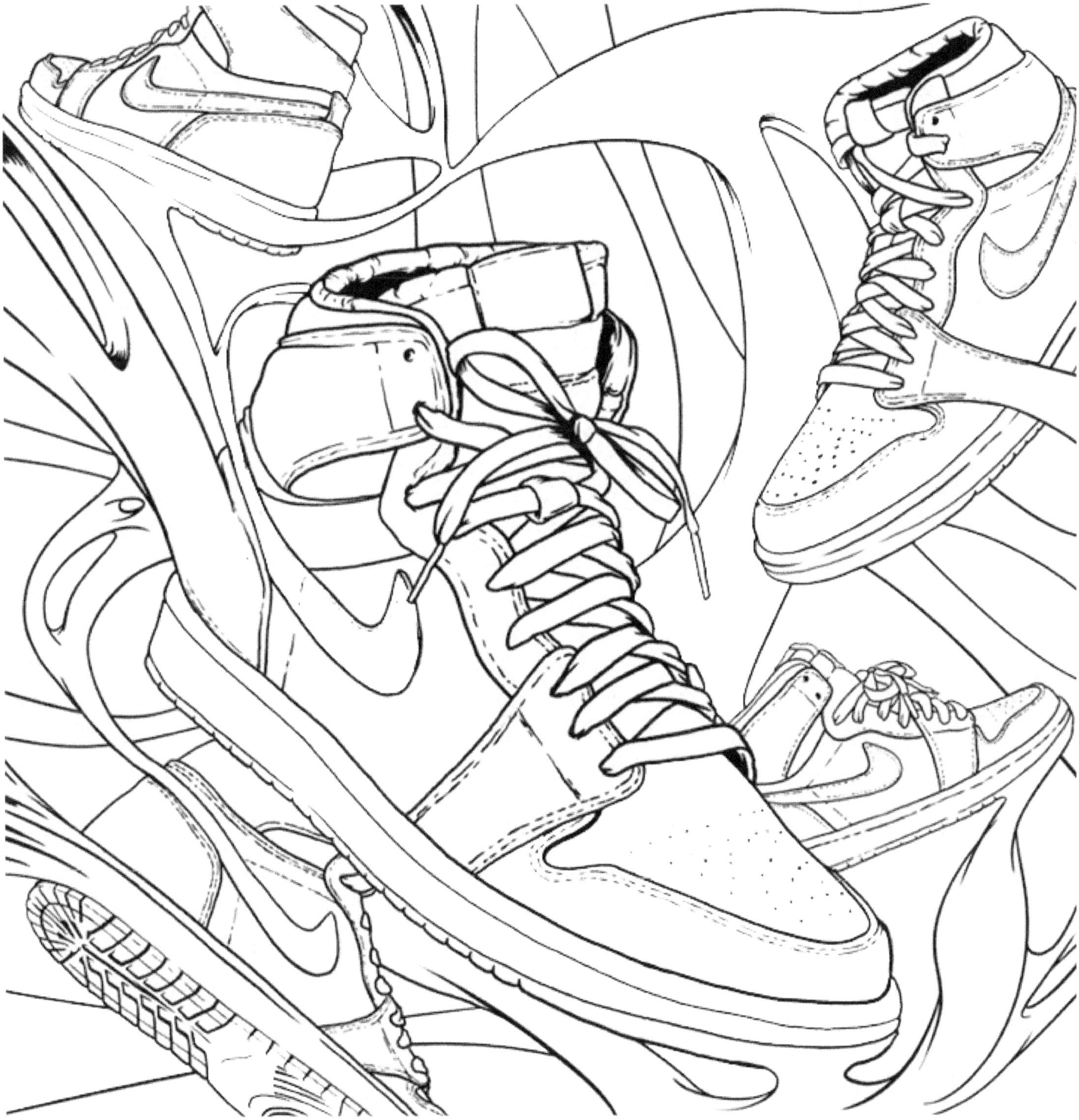

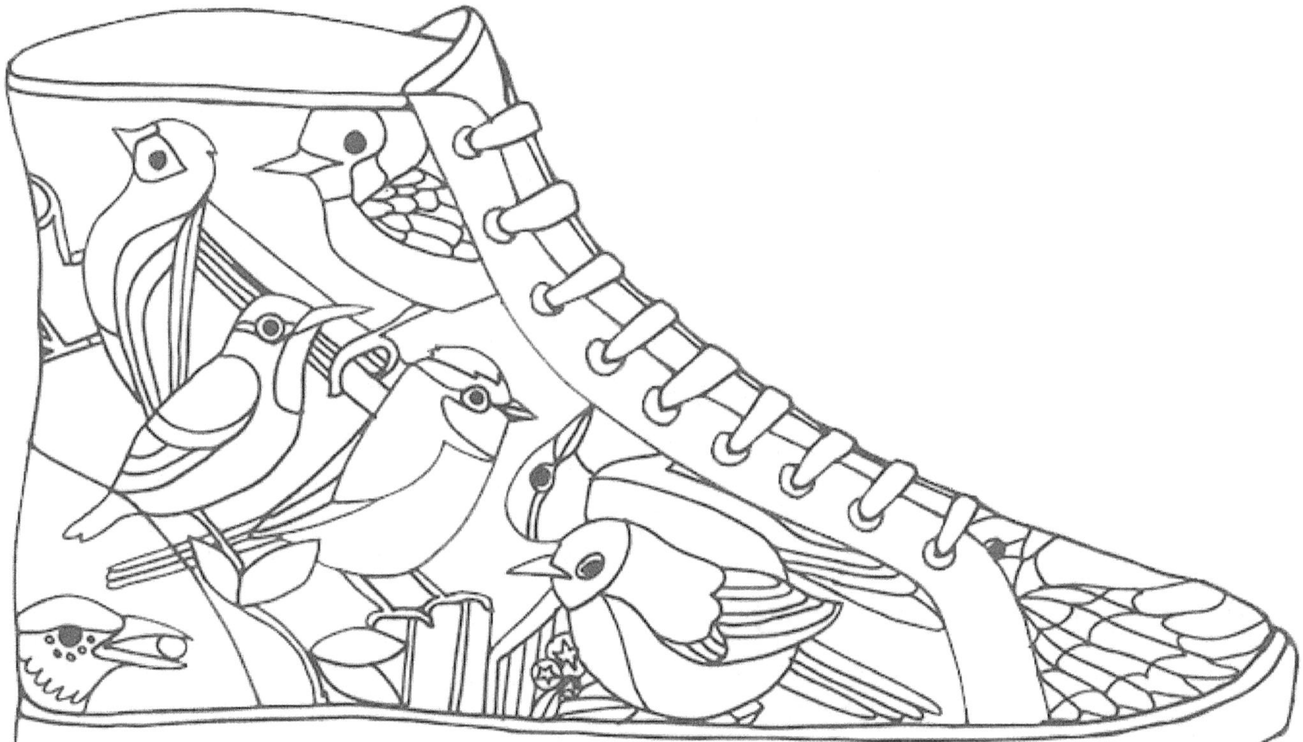

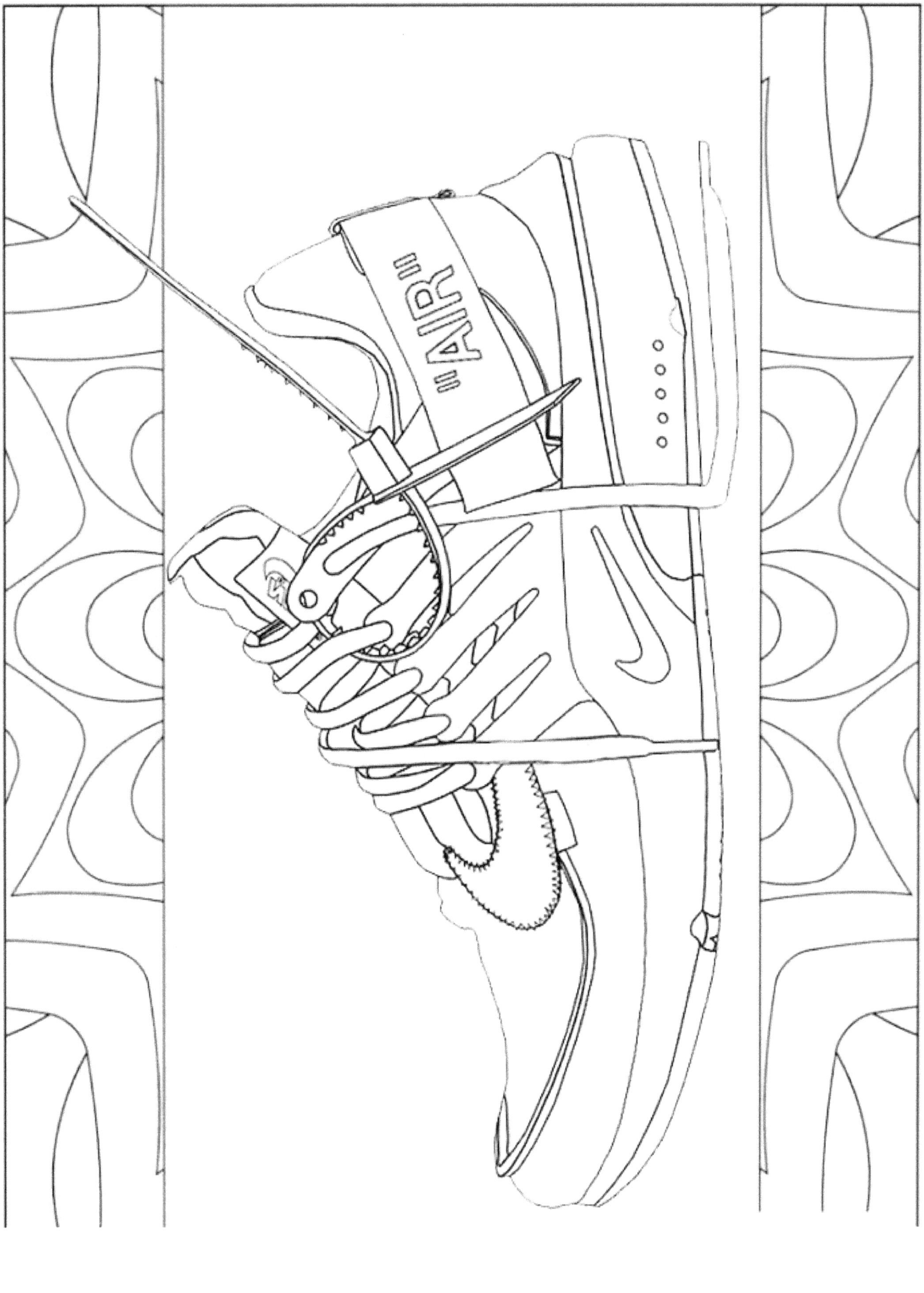
"AIR"

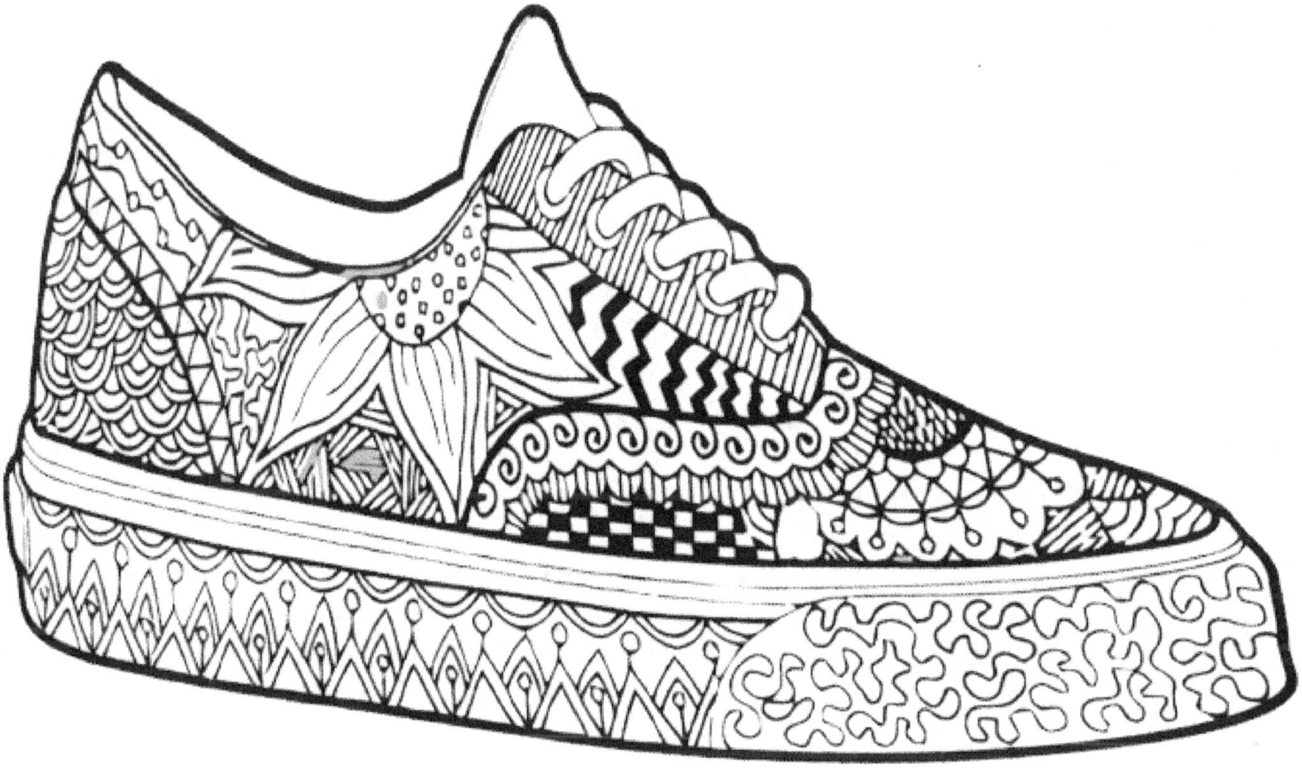

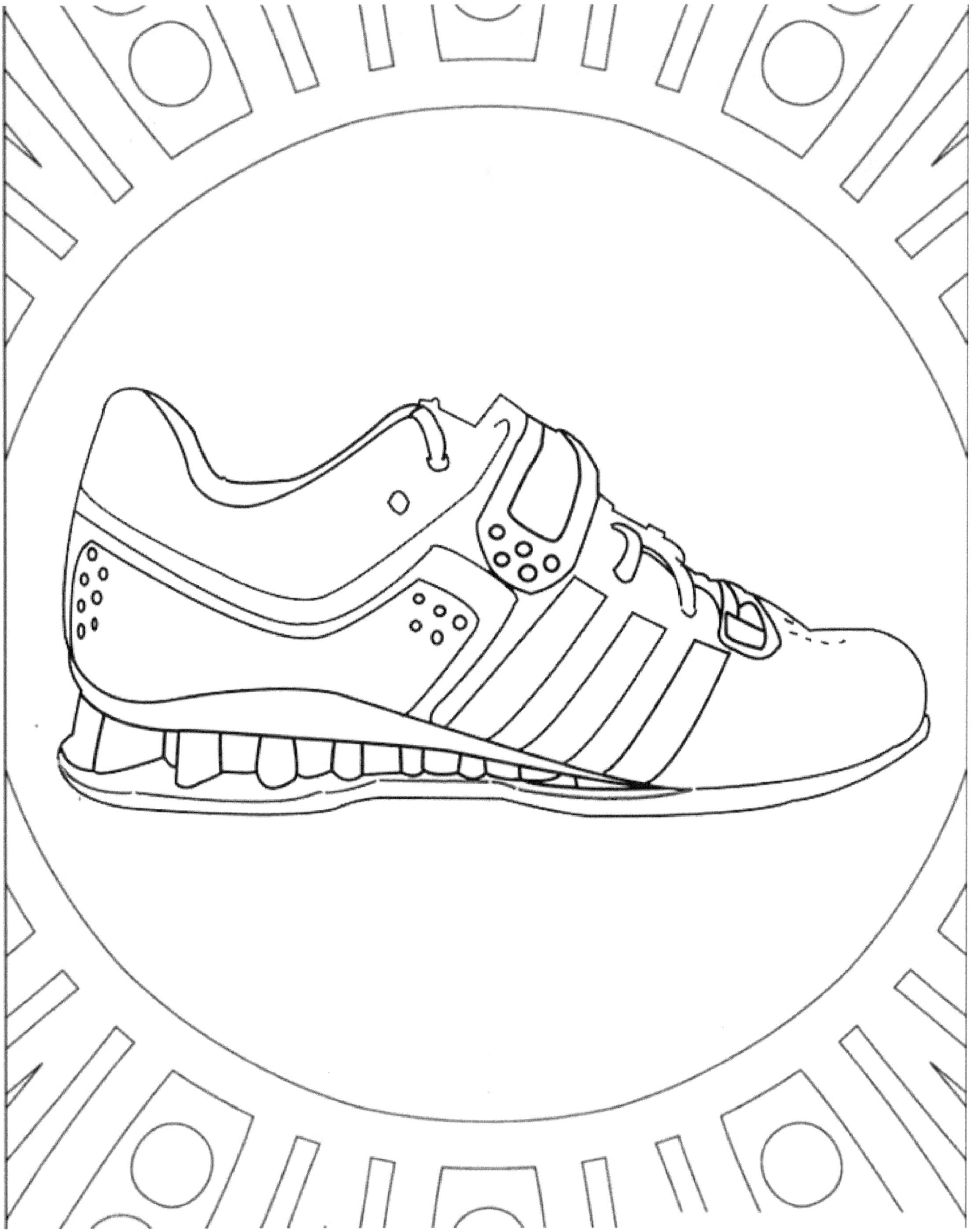

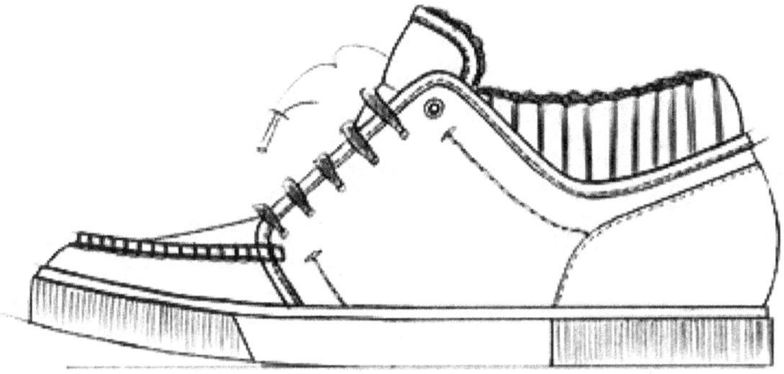

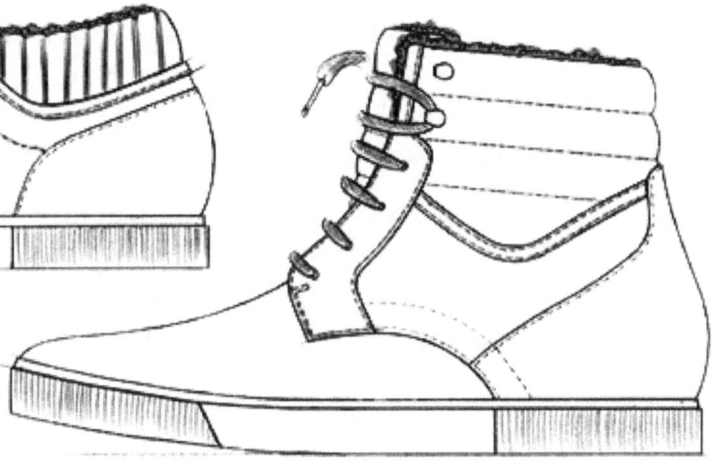

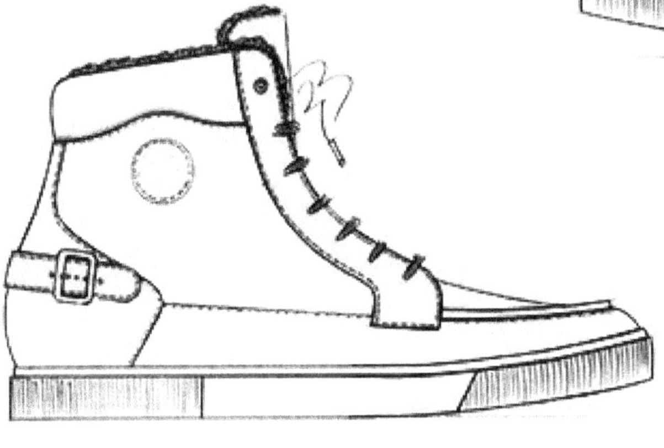

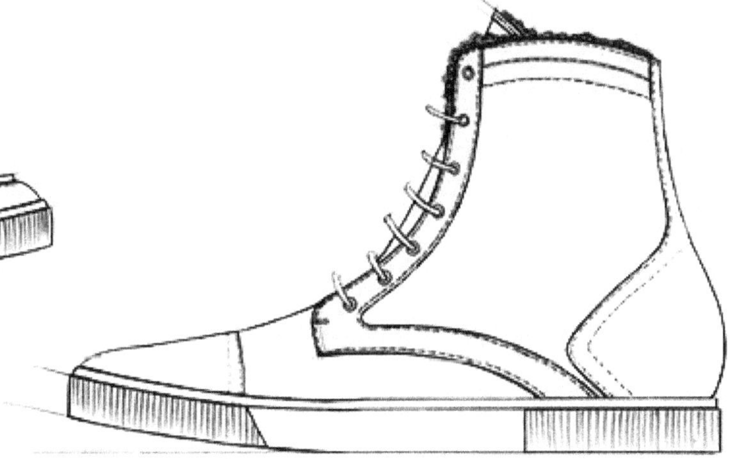

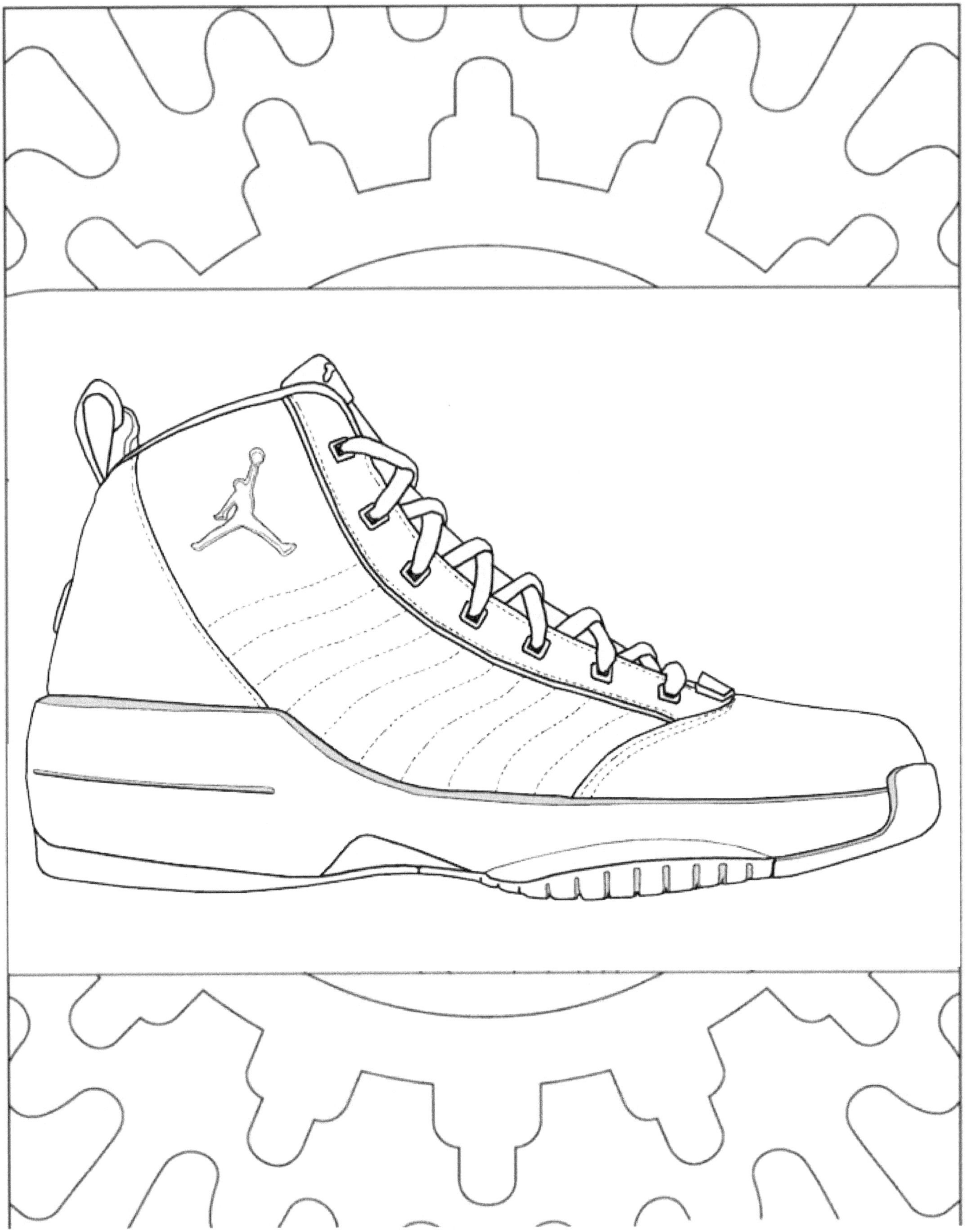

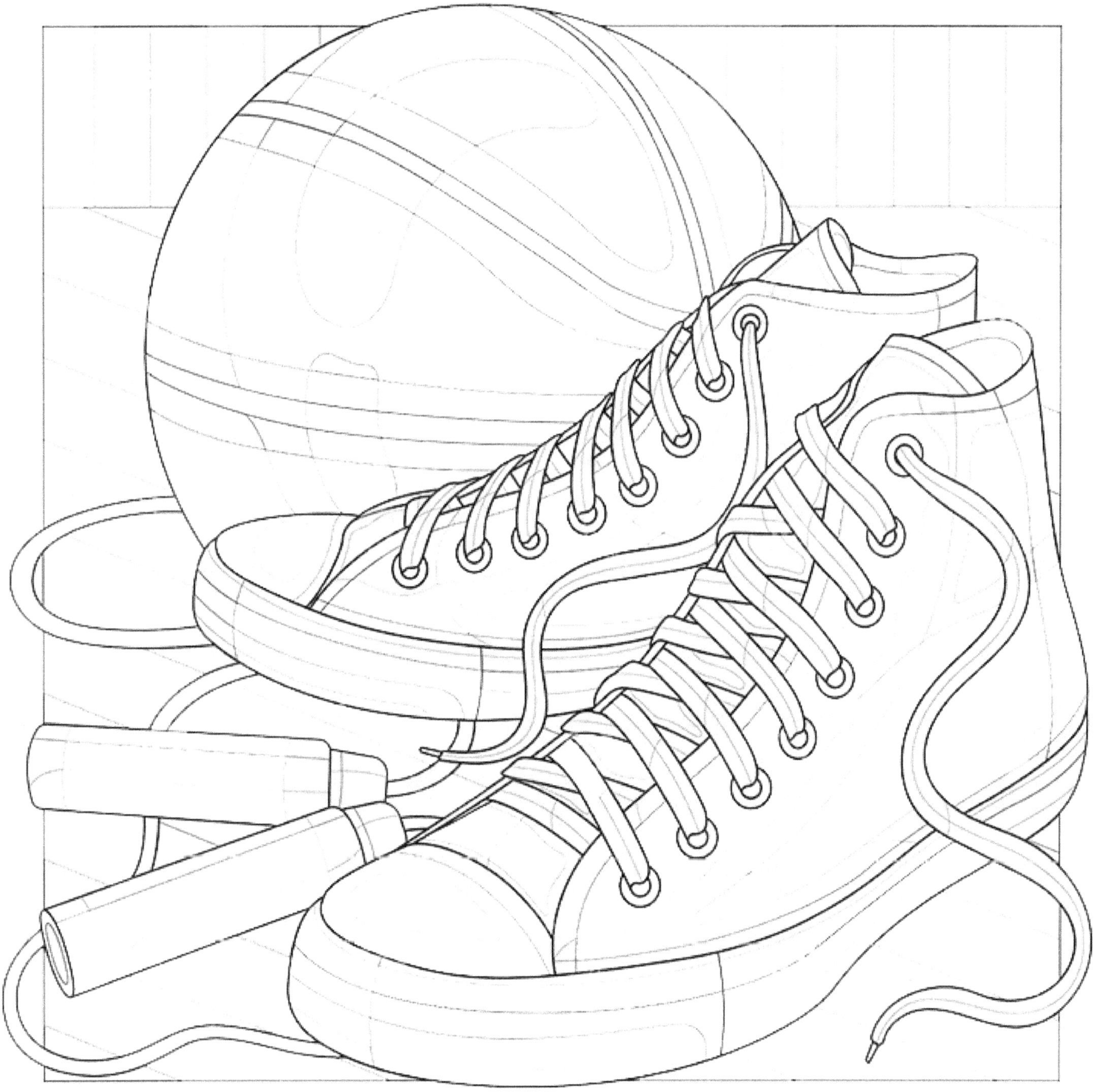

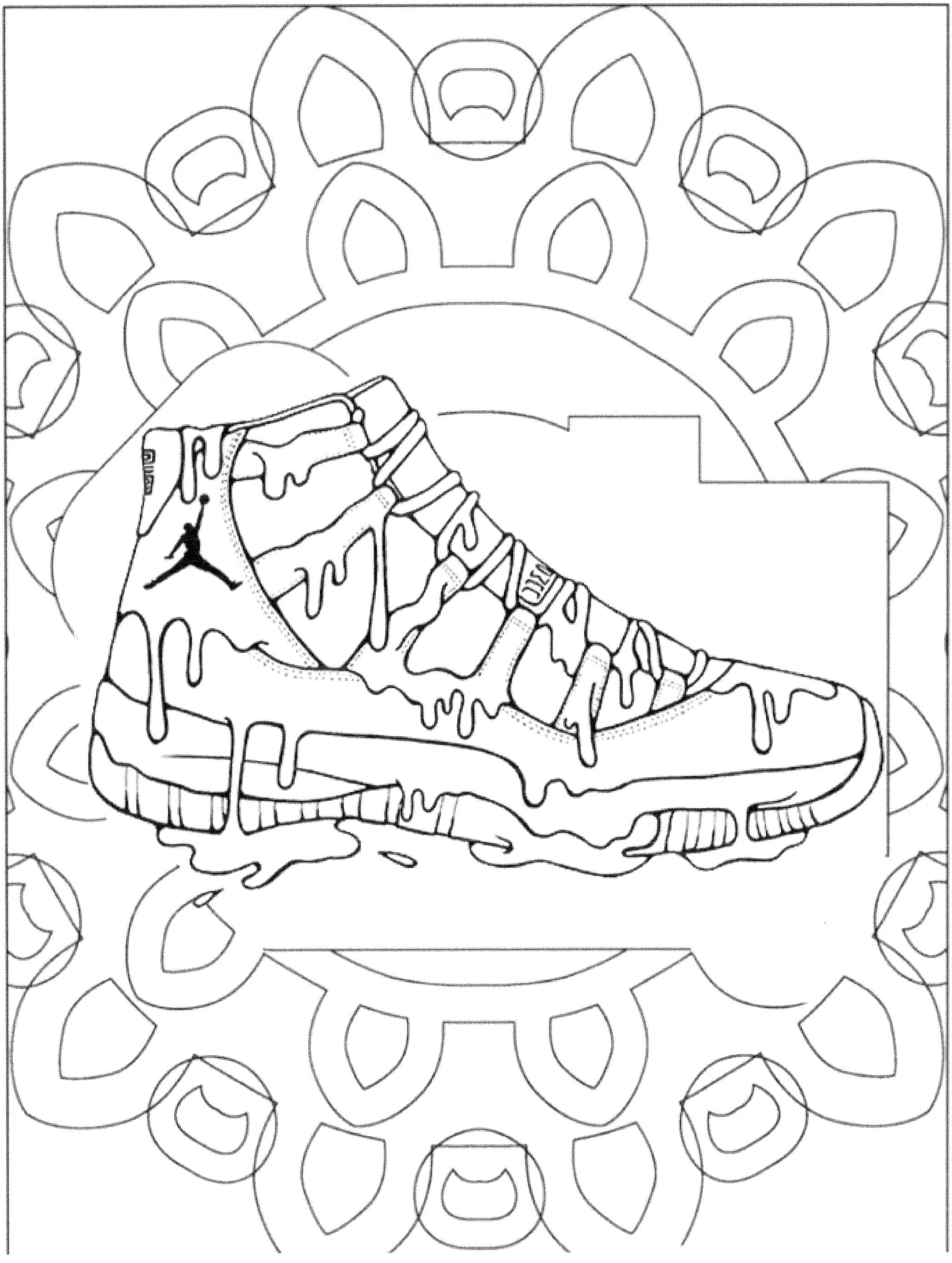

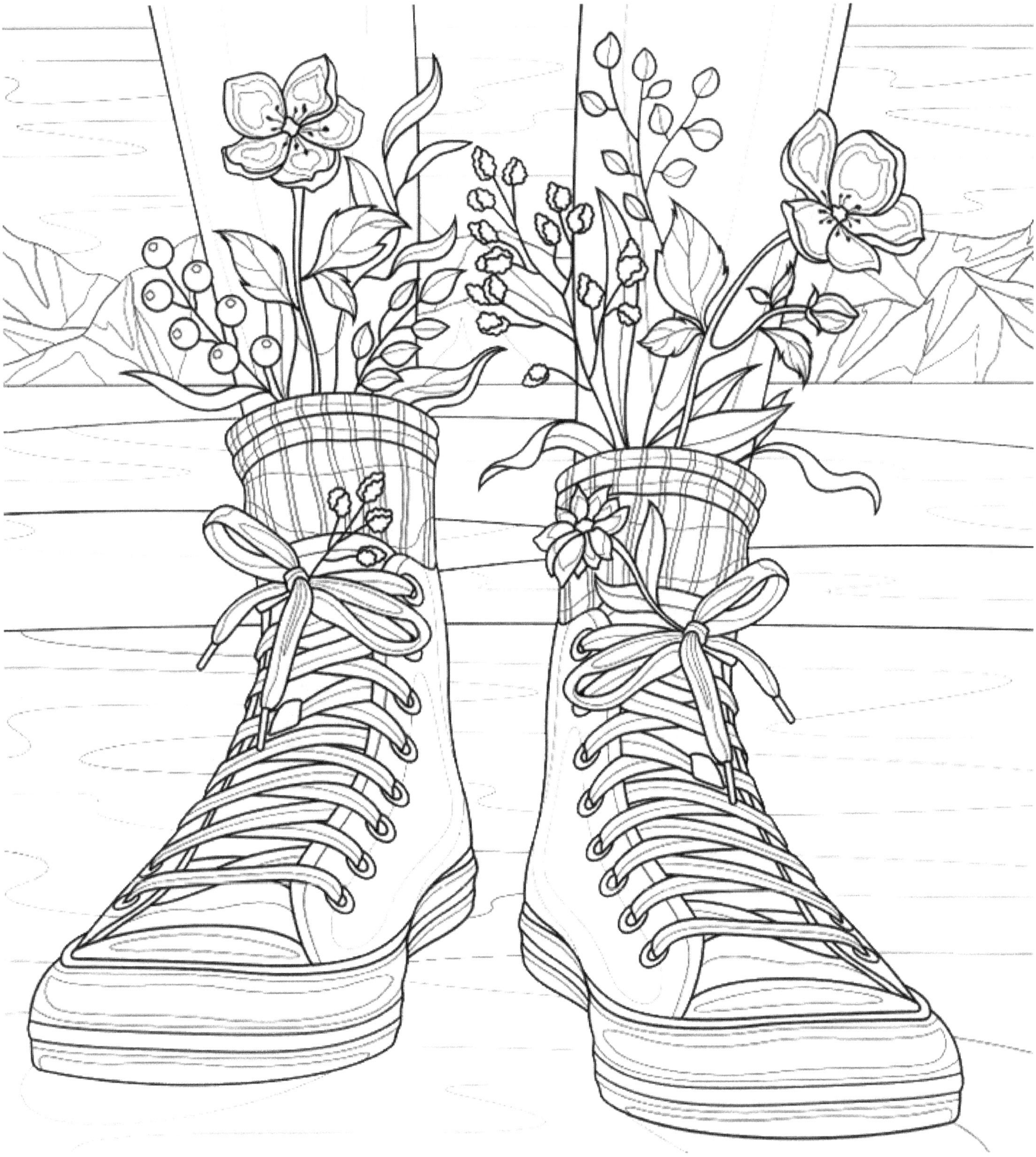

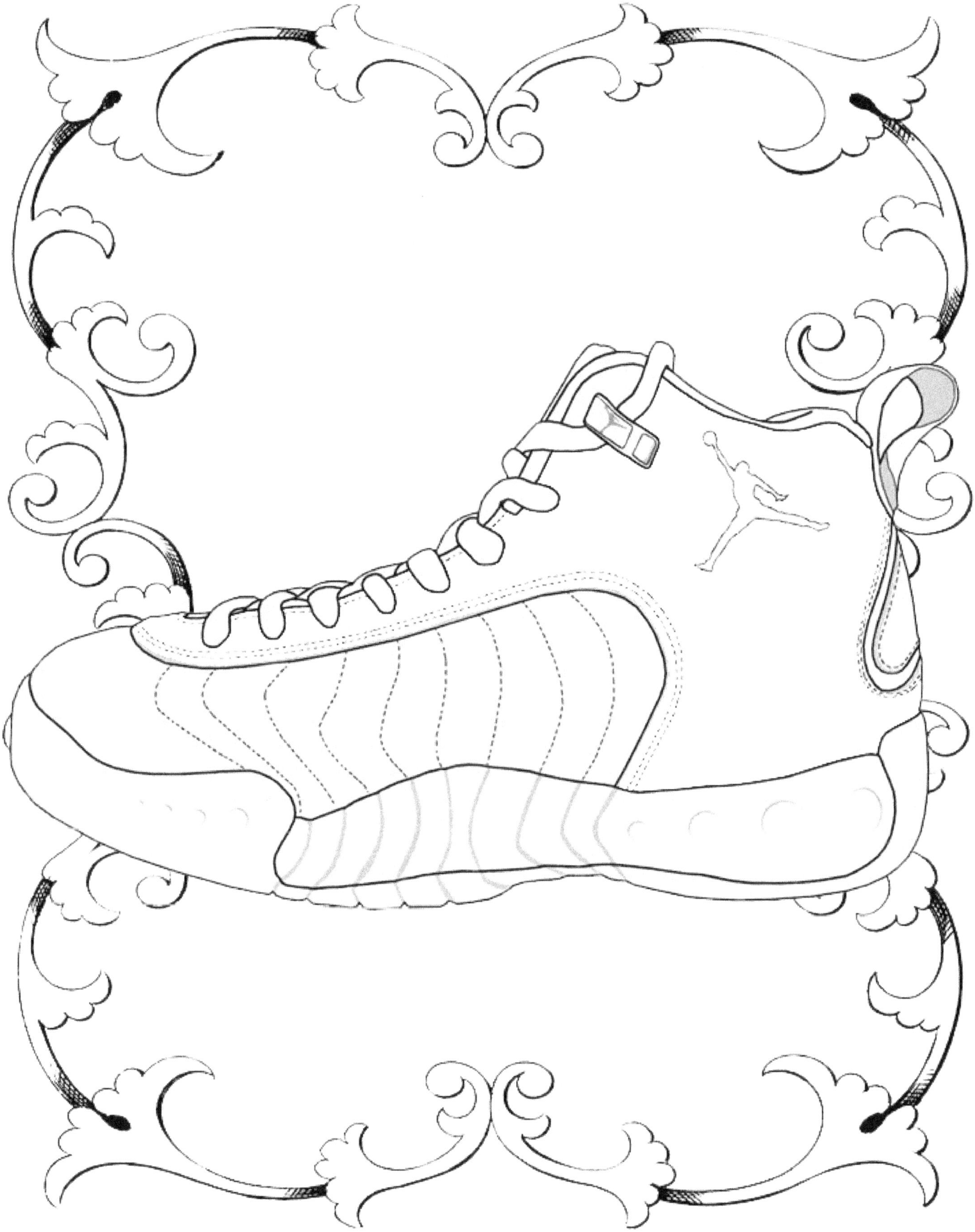

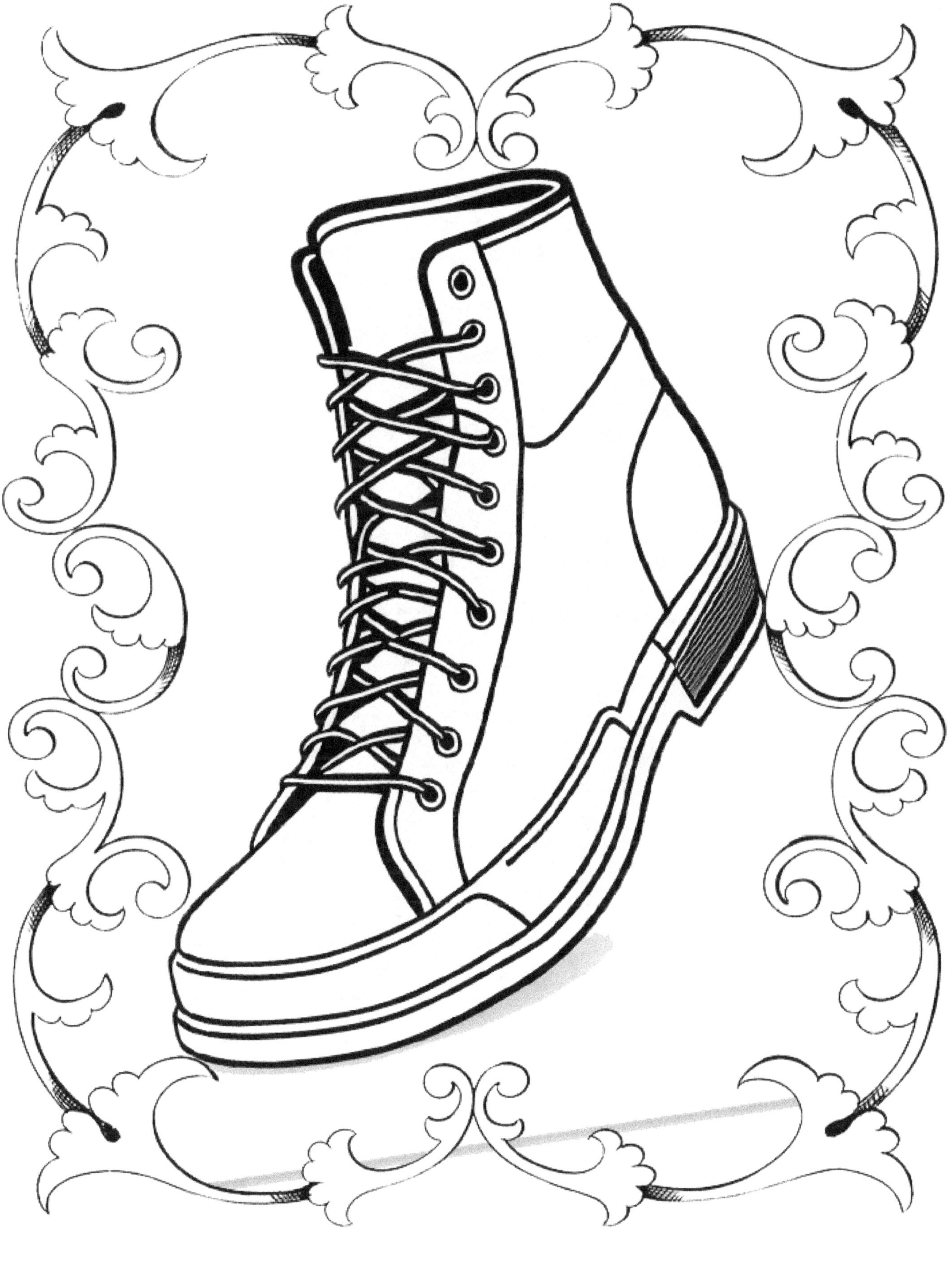

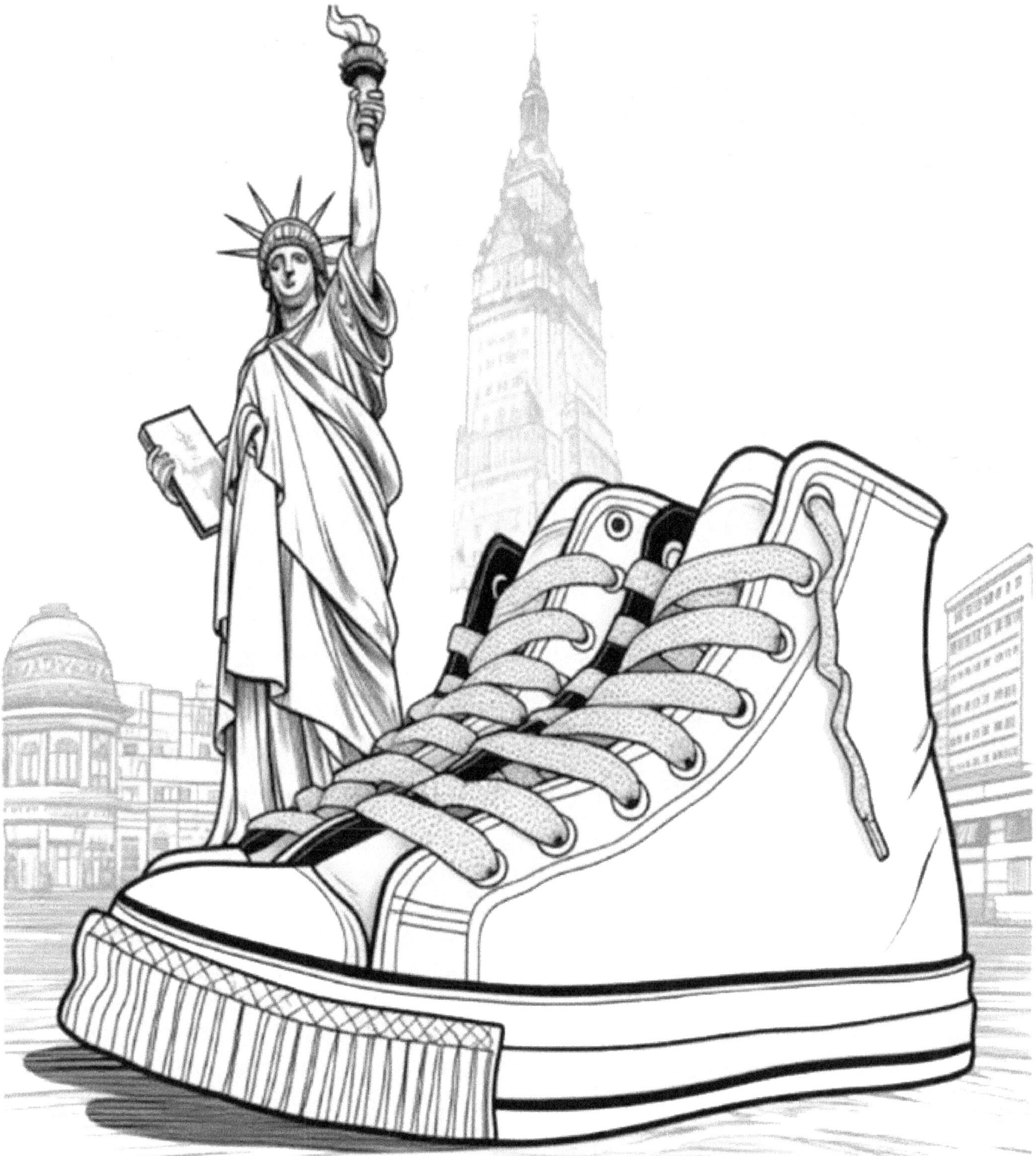

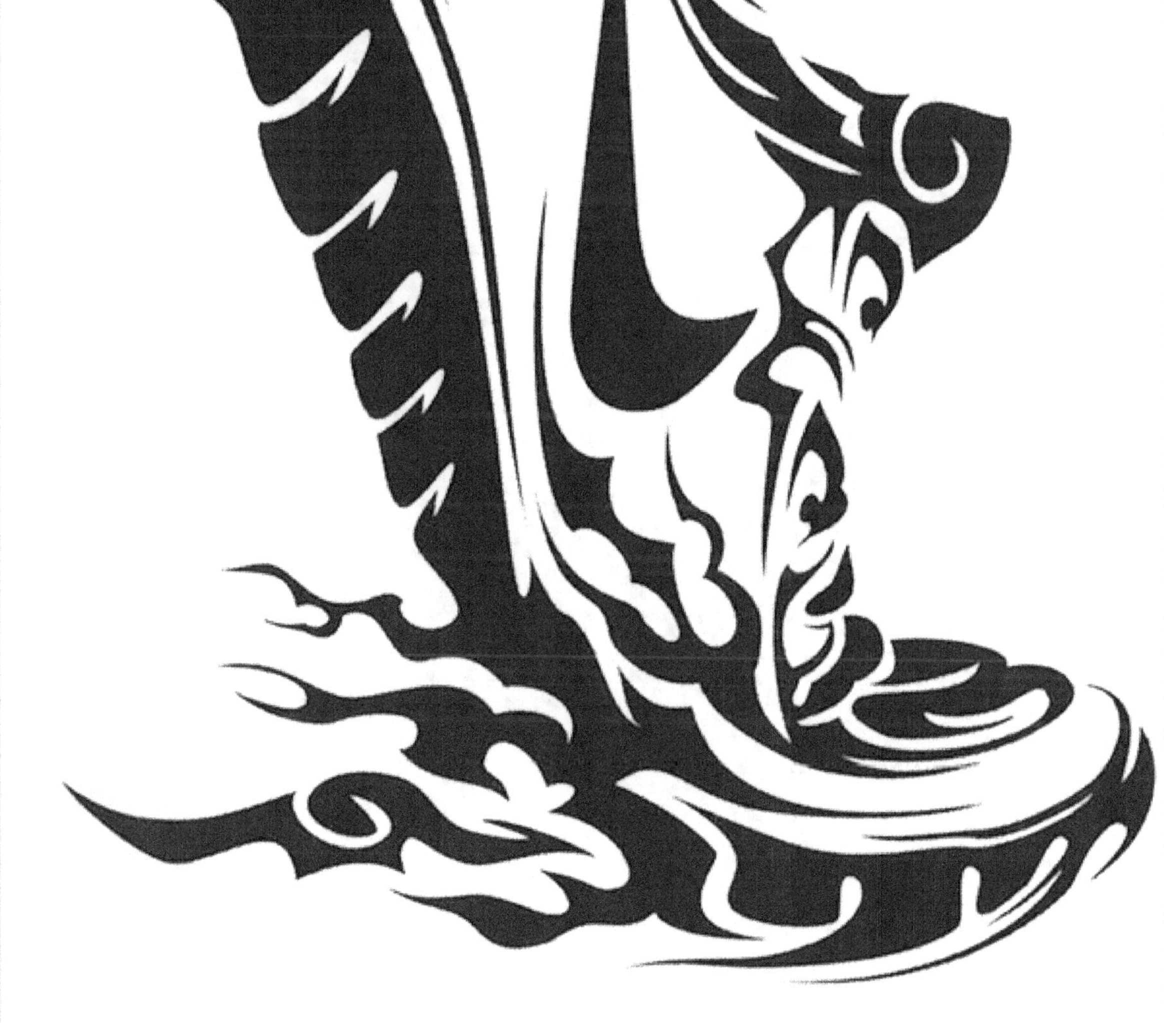

www.ingramcontent.com/pod-product-compliance
Lightning Source LLC
Chambersburg PA
CBHW082144290526
45794CB00008B/3155
9798853684904